ENGLISH MEDIEVAL BOROUGHS

ENGLISH MEDIEVAL BOROUGHS

A HAND-LIST

M. W. BERESFORD

Professor of Economic History in
the University of Leeds

and

H. P. R. FINBERG

Professor Emeritus of English Local History
in the University of Leicester

ROWMAN AND LITTLEFIELD
TOTOWA, NEW JERSEY

First published in the United States, 1973, by
Rowman and Littlefield, Totowa, N.J.

© M. W. Beresford 1973

Library of Congress Cataloging in Publication Data

Beresford, Maurice Warwick, 1920–
    English medieval boroughs.

    Includes bibliographical references.
    1. Boroughs—Great Britain. 2. Great Britain—
Administrative and political divisions. I. Finberg,
H. P. R., joint author. II. Title.
JS3265.B47   914.2   73–6776
ISBN 0–87471–201–7

Printed in Great Britain

Motto

As to your town, no doubt it was ancient, but not quite so old as the Flood, Babel, Babylon or Rome. The inhabitants are not the worse for not having long pedigrees of Roman blood in their veins; they may be contented with a descent no earlier than the Normans.

J. Waylen. *Chronicle of the Devizes*, 1839, 22

PREFACE

Professor Finberg began to publish his findings on the origin of certain boroughs a quarter of a century ago.[1] More recently I myself have made a particular type of burghality, the planted town, the principal object of my research for nearly a decade.[2] When Professor Finberg retired from his chair at Leicester under the inexorable rules of academic superannuation, which bear no relation to a scholar's capacity and inclination for continued work, it suited both of us to join forces and draw up a provisional list of all those places in England that could claim to have been a borough at one time or another in the Middle Ages. The University of Leeds provided funds to make our collaboration possible, and that assistance is gratefully acknowledged. Professor Finberg desires me to add that he is not responsible for the editorial presentation of the gazetteer, in which the publishers have followed their house style.

M.W.B.

Authors and publishers acknowledge assistance from the University of Leeds Publications Fund

[1] H. P. R. Finberg. 'The Borough of Tavistock', *Trans Devon Assocn*, LXXIX, 1947, 129–53; 'The Boroughs of Devon', *Devon and Cornwall Notes and Queries*, XXIV, 1951, 203–9, and XXVII, 1956, 27–8; *Gloucestershire Studies*, 1957, 52–88.

[2] M. W. Beresford. 'The Six New Towns of the Bishops of Winchester', *Med Archaeol*, III, 1959, 187–215; *New Towns of the Middle Ages*, 1967.

CONTENTS

9

AUTHORS' ACKNOWLEDGEMENTS

Beds: Miss Joyce Godber; *Bucks:* Mrs E. M. Elvey; *Cambs:* Mr J. Ravensdale; *Cheshire:* Mr B. C. Redwood; *Cornwall:* Mr P. L. Hull, Dr R. E. Witherick; *Cumberland and Westmorland:* Mr B. C. Jones; *Devon:* Mr H. S. A. Fox, Prof W. G. Hoskins, Mrs A. M. Erskine, Mr W. Best Harris, Mr N. S. E. Pugsley, Mr P. A. Kennedy; *Dorset:* Miss M. Holmes, Mr C. Taylor; *Durham:* Mr M. G. Snape, Mrs Jean Scammell; *Essex:* Mr K. C. Newton, Dr R. H. Britnell, Miss Hilda Grieve, Mr B. S. Smith, Mr P. A. Couzens; *Hants:* Miss S. D. Thomson, Miss P. E. Clifford, Mrs E. Cottrill, Mr M. J. W. Willis-Fear; *Herefords:* Miss E. M. Jancey, Mr A. Shaw Wright, Mr F. Noble, Mr J. G. Hillaby; *Herts:* Mr P. Walne; *Hunts:* Mr P. G. M. Dickinson; *Kent:* Mr D. E. Collins, Mr F. Hull; *Lancs:* Mr Horton; *Leics:* Dr L. A. Parker; *Lincs:* Mrs J. Varley, Mr E. J. Redshaw, Mr E. Gillett; *Middlesex:* Mr W. J. Smith; *Norfolk:* Miss J. M. Kennedy, Mr Paul Rutledge; *Northumberland:* Dr C. M. Fraser, Mr W. Young, Mr M. G. Snape; *Notts:* Dr A. Rogers; *Oxon:* Mrs M. D. Lobel, Mr G. G. Burkitt; *Shropshire:* Miss M. C. Hill, the late Mr J. L. Hobbs; *Somerset:* Mr R. J. E. Bush, Miss E. A. Hatch; *Staffs:* Dr D. M. Palliser, Dr P. and Dr M. Spufford, Mr R. Frost, Mr C. C. Taylor, Mr S. C. Newton; *Suffolk:* Mr D. Charman; *Surrey:* Miss M. Gollancz, Miss E. M. Dance, Mr Peter Gwyn; *Sussex:* Mr C. G. Holland; *Warws:* Mrs E. A. Gooder, Dr B. K. Roberts, Mr W. H. Hosford, Dr L. Fox, Mr M. W. Farr, Mr A. A. Dibben; *Wilts:* Prof R. B. Pugh, Mr M. G. Rathbone; *Worcs:* Prof R. H. Hilton, Mr W. A. Taylor, Mr E. H. Sargeant; *Yorks:* Prof J. H. Le Patourel, Mr J. W. Cox, Miss Meredith, Mr N. Higson, Mr J. M. Collinson. *General:* Dr R. E. Glasscock.

The tables were compiled by Mr B. J. Barber and the manuscript typed by Mrs Maureen Gorman.

LIST OF TABLES

LIST OF ABBREVIATIONS AND SHORT TITLES OF WORKS CITED

Baker, *Northants*	G. Baker. *The History and Antiquities of Northamptonshire*, 2 vols, 1822–41
Ballard	A. Ballard. *British Borough Charters, 1042–1216*, 1913
Ballard & Tait	A. Ballard & J. Tait. *British Borough Charters, 1216–1307*, 1923
Bede, *Hist Eccl*	Bede. *Ecclesiastical History of the English Nation*
Birch, *Cart Sax*	W. de G. Birch. *Cartularium Saxonicum*, 3 vols, 1885–93
Book of Fees	PRO. *The Book of Fees*, 3 vols, 1921–31
BM	British Museum
C	See key to PRO call numbers, p 19
Cal Ancient Deeds	PRO. *Ancient Deeds: Descriptive Catalogue*, 6 vols, 1890–1915
Cal Charter Rolls	PRO. *Calendar of Charter Rolls*, 6 vols, 1903–27
Cal Close Rolls	PRO. *Calendar of Close Rolls*, 64 vols, 1892–1963
Cal Inq Misc	PRO. *Calendar of Miscellaneous Inquisitions*, 7 vols, 1916–69
Cal Inq Post Mortem	PRO. *Calendar of Inquisitions Post Mortem*, 15 vols, 1904–69
Cal Pat Rolls	PRO. *Calendar of Patent Rolls*, 68 vols, 1891–1969
Crawford Charters	A. S. Napier & W. H. Stevenson, eds. *The Crawford Collection of Early Charters and Documents now in the Bodleian Library*, 1895
Curia Regis Rolls	PRO. *Curia Regis Rolls*, 15 vols, 1925–69
DB	*Domesday Book* (original vols and foliation)
DL	See key to PRO call numbers, p 19
Dugdale, *Monasticon*	Sir William Dugdale. *Monasticon Anglicanum*, eds J. Caley, H. Ellis & B. Bandinel, 8 vols, 1817–30

List of Abbreviations and Short Titles of Works Cited

E	See key to PRO call numbers, p 19
EHR	*English Historical Review*
Eyton, *Shropshire*	R. W. Eyton. *Antiquities of Shropshire*, 12 vols, 1854–60
Glos Inq pm	British Record Society. *Gloucestershire Inquisitions post Mortem*, 6 vols, 1893–9, and 1903–14
HMC	Historical Manuscripts Commission. *Reports*
Hutchins, *Dorset*	J. Hutchins. *History and Antiquities of Dorset*, 4 vols, 1861–70
JI	See key to PRO call numbers, p 19
KB	See key to PRO call numbers, p 19
Kemble, *Codex Diplomaticus*	J. M. Kemble. *Codex Diplomaticus*, 6 vols, 1838–46
Lysons, *Devon*	D. & S. Lysons. *Magna Britannia*, pt 8, 1822
Morant, *Essex*	P. Morant. *The History and Antiquities of the county of Essex*, 2 vols, 1768
Northumberland County History	*A History of Northumberland*, various editors, 14 vols, 1893–1940
Ormerod, *Cheshire*	G. Ormerod. *History of the County Palatine and City of Chester*, 3 vols, 1875–82
Pipe Roll, ed Hunter	J. Hunter, ed. *Magnus Rotulus Scaccarii de anno 31°· Henrici I*, 1833 *The Great Roll of the Pipe.... for 1155–1158*, 1844 *The Great Roll of the Pipe for 1188–1189*, 1844
Pipe Roll Soc	Pipe Roll Society Publications
Placita de Quo Warranto	W. Illingworth, ed. *Placita de quo Warranto temp. Edward I, II, et III, in curia receptae scaccarii Westm. asservata*, 1818
Placitorum Abbreviatio	G. Rose & W. Illingworth, eds. *Abbreviatio Placitorum, Richard I–Edward II*, 1811
PRO	Public Record Office, London
Raine, *North Durham*	J. Raine. *The History and Antiquities of North Durham*, 1852
Regesta Regum Anglo-Normannorum	H. W. C. Davis, H. A. Cronne & R. H. C. Davis, eds. *Regesta Regum Anglo-Normannorum*, 4 vols, 1913–69
Robertson, *Anglo-Saxon Charters*	A. J. Robertson. *Anglo-Saxon Charters*, 1939

List of Abbreviations and Short Titles of Works Cited

Rot Chart	T. D. Hardy, ed. *Rotuli Chartarum in Turri Londinensi Asservati*, 1837
Rot Lit Claus	T. D. Hardy, ed. *Rotuli Litterarum Clausarum in Turri Londinensi Asservati*, 2 vols, 1833, 1844
Rotuli Hundredorum	W. Illingworth, ed. *Rotuli Hundredorum temp. Hen. III et Edw. I in Turr' Lond' et in curia receptae scaccarii Westm. asservati*, 2 vols, 1812, 1818
Rot Parl	J. Strachey, J. Pridden & E. Upham, eds. *Rotuli Parliamentorum*, 6 vols, 1767–83
SC	See key to PRO call numbers, p 19
Staffs Hist Coll	William Salt Archaeological Society. *Collections for a History of Staffordshire*
Taxatio Ecclesiastica	S. Ayscough & J. Caley, eds. *Taxatio Ecclesiastica Angliae et Walliae*, 1802
VCH	*Victoria History of the Counties of England* (in progress)
Weinbaum	Martin Weinbaum. *British Borough Charters, 1307–1660*, 1943
Willard	J. F. Willard. 'Taxation Boroughs and Parliamentary Boroughs' in J. G. Edwards, ed. *Historical Essays in Honour of James Tait*, 1933, 417–35

CALL NUMBERS FOR CLASSES OF DOCUMENT CITED FROM THE PUBLIC RECORD OFFICE

C2	Chancery Proceedings, Series I
C47	Chancery Miscellanea
C52	Chancery, Cartae Antiquae Rolls
C132	Inquisitions Post Mortem, Chancery Series I, Henry III
C133	Ibid, Edward I
C134	Ibid, Edward II
C135	Ibid, Edward III
C136	Ibid, Richard II
C143	Inquisitions ad quod damnum
C145	Miscellaneous Inquisitions
DL29	Duchy of Lancaster, Ministers' Accounts
DL43	Duchy of Lancaster, Rentals and Surveys
E40	Ancient Deeds, Series A
E142	Ancient Extents
E179	Subsidy Rolls, etc
E326	Ancient Deeds, Series B
E364	Exchequer, Rolls of Foreign Accounts, Pipe Office
E372	Exchequer, LTR Pipe Rolls
JI 1	Justices Itinerant, Assize Rolls, Eyre Rolls, etc
KB26	King's (Queen's) Bench, Curia Regis Rolls
SC 1	Special Collections: Ancient Correspondence
SC 2	Ibid, Court Rolls
SC 11	Ibid, Rentals and Surveys, Rolls
SC 12	Ibid, Rentals and Surveys, Portfolios

INTRODUCTION

1 Aims of the List

The purpose of our *List* is a simple one—to contribute to the history of English medieval boroughs by providing, for the first time, a gazetteer of places which in their day were reckoned to be boroughs. The symptoms of burghality are various in their nature and incidence and we therefore devote a section of this Introduction to the matter of sources and authentication. Our *List* includes virtually all English county towns and very many others that are still called boroughs. The vicissitudes of economic change in the post-medieval centuries have weakened the position of some entrants to our catalogue, and their burghality is no longer exercised. Some of these boroughs, like the parliamentary boroughs of Grampound and Old Sarum, were extinguished in circumstances that bring them to the attention of almost every schoolboy whose history lessons include the Reform Act and the Municipal Corporations Act. The burghality of others was extinguished well before 1832, but in circumstances so placid that no record of the occasion has survived. Some others, a small number, are known not to have survived even the Middle Ages; and a few were—as far as can be seen—totally abortive, their burghality a necessary but clearly not a sufficient part of their founder's endowment. On the other hand, a few of our medieval boroughs lapsed but were revived: there is nothing in Charles I's charter to Leeds to suggest that the charter of 1207 was then remembered, and Queen Victoria's charter to Bradford assumed that borough privileges were being conveyed for the first time, forgetting that the Queen's ancestors, as dukes of Lancaster, had happily augmented their revenues from the rents of burgage plots in Bradford.

Our own *List* deals only with medieval burghality, and we have drawn the line at creations and recreations that occurred after 1509: the rare occasions when a date after 1509 appears in our pages will arise where the only reference to burgages, etc, occurs in a post-medieval document but without any Tudor charter or letters patent to explain the burghality; in these circumstances we have thought it reasonable to imply a medieval grant of privileges.[1]

2 Relation to Previous Work

At first sight it might seem surprising that no list of medieval English boroughs has hitherto been compiled, for, as Dr G. H. Martin has recently reminded us, there have been general and particular histories of English municipalities for well over a century.[2] Once Ballard had begun to publish his dissection of extant borough charters in 1913 there was clearly little incentive for anyone else to begin an independent search,[3] although it was to be 10 years before Tait's continuation of Ballard's work[4] took the charter material to 1272 and 20 more years before Dr Weinbaum extended the survey beyond the end of the Middle Ages.[5] The form of Ballard's book, followed by Tait and Weinbaum, was dictated by its prime aim of analysing the subject matter of borough charters: the existence and provenance of the charters was a subsidiary matter, but each author provided an alphabetical list of the boroughs concerned, and an indication of where each charter could be found. The subsidiary nature of this material in the three authors' eyes is perhaps indicated by the smallness of the print that the Cambridge University Press gave to these references.

It is a tribute to the work of many local and county historians in the generations before Ballard and Tait's books that so many of the latter's references lead the reader to printed versions of borough charters rather than to archival sources. Systematic publication of the text of medieval borough charters had begun as early as 1837 with T. D. Hardy's edition[6] of the charters that were enrolled in Chancery between 1199 and 1216. In 1903 the Public Record Office began to publish its *Calendar* of the same series of enrolments,[7] beginning in 1226 (there being no enrolments during the minority of Henry III, 1216–26), and by 1916 these had been taken as far as 1417, a date by which new borough creations were becoming rare. In addition to these published charters and others disclosed by the *Calendar* of the Patent Rolls, Ballard and

Tait were able to profit from another consequence of the late nine-teenth-century interest in municipal origins—the searches among the muniments of the older corporations that were carried out for the Historical Manuscripts Commission and embodied in their *Reports*.[8] Since these searches had descended to minor and, in some cases, to near-defunct municipalities, it was not unnatural for the impression to gain ground that the corpus of English boroughs was complete, an impression emphasised by the appearance in 1936 of James Tait's magisterial study, *The Medieval English Borough*.

Certainly the harvest gathered in by Ballard and Tait was con-siderable, as evidenced by the large number of boroughs in our *List* with the references 'Ballard' or 'Ballard & Tait' indicating that the earliest evidence for burghality is still a charter tabulated and analysed in one of their volumes. Yet we have been able to go further, ending with more than 600 places that have a claim to medieval burghality. The principal reason for the additional entries is, of course, that Ballard and Tait were concerned with a narrower objective, the con-tent of borough charters.

In their scheme of work a borough without a charter text to study was irrelevant, but our more limited aim, the identification of bur-ghality, necessarily leads us to many places where no charter at all can be traced. Ballard had already encountered the mortality of charters. Eight boroughs, for example, that were in existence by 1086 lost their first charters and had no documentary proof of their liberties earlier than 1140. No Welsh borough founded before 1223 had its original charter surviving.

For the absence of an extant charter there are several possible explana-tions: before the Chancery began its enrolment of charters in 1199 there was nowhere for a grantor, whether king or subject, to place the grant firmly on record except in the charter itself and, precious as its liberties were, a piece of parchment had no guarantee of preservation in per-petuity. When even great towns have failed to preserve their early medieval charters, it is not surprising that smaller towns have no early evidences. Even after 1199 it was prudence and convenience, not the force of law, that led to the enrolment of charters on Chancery rolls, and there are well attested boroughs of considerable size without

charters either on the Charter Rolls or on the Patent Rolls. The latter
series, beginning in 1201, had a wider scope of subject matter than the
Charter Rolls but some grants of burghal privileges are to be found
there.[9]

Again, it is not surprising that petty lords who had created petty
boroughs on their demesnes did not always go to the cost and trouble
of obtaining an enrolment in Chancery, and the more petty the
borough the less likely for it to have any place where its muniments
might be expected to survive to modern times. Even if the seigneur
retained a copy of the charter among his own muniments, its loss is not
remarkable in view of the small bulk remaining from the records of
medieval manors compared with what must once have existed. Nor
indeed is it certain that a petty borough was always initiated by a written
charter: practice was more important than parchment, and an oral
grant and an appropriate recognition of burghers and burgage tenure
by the seigneur and his officers could be sufficient.

Apart from its survival in the original or as enrolled, the grant of a
borough charter may occasionally be evidenced indirectly. Most frequent of these indirect evidences is a record of a payment to the king
for having a charter or for confirming one, and for these evidences we
must turn to the Pipe Rolls of the Exchequer. The publication of this
great series[10] (which began earlier than the Charter Rolls) had been
carried to the roll of 1186-7 by 1915, but, giving no text of a charter,
this source did not contribute to Ballard & Tait's compilation. It was
only after the New Series was inaugurated by Lady Stenton in 1925
that reasonable indexing of borough references began.[11] Even in 1971
publication of the Pipe Rolls has reached only 1215-16, and the sheer
bulk of the manuscript Rolls and, after 1216, the absence of contemporary indexes make the search for casual references to burgages and
borough charters a daunting one, too daunting, it must be confessed,
for the present authors. References to the unprinted Pipe Rolls, where
they do occur in our List, are the result of chance finds and not systematic searches.

The authentication of burghality subsequent to Ballard & Tait's
work is mainly, as our references show, through the discovery of new
indirect evidences rather than of charters unknown to them. Where new

charters have come to light, it is usually because archival sources are now open that were not available to scholars earlier in the century. The proliferation of county record offices and the assembly of private records within them have contributed most of the additions, although some are due to the listing of private archives by the National Register and to publication by local record societies. A very small number has emerged from local municipal archives as a result of a more professional scrutiny by their archivists than was possible earlier in the century. Mention must also be made of the new charter material, only a small fraction of it concerned with burghality, brought together for the period 1066–1154 by H. W. C. Davis, H. A. Cronne and R. H. C. Davis.[12] Altogether, there is charter material for some 200 of the 609 places in our *List*, and indirect evidence of charters for another 15 (see Table 10). For the remaining 400 cases, the evidence on which we have claimed burghality is of a different nature, and the next section of the Introduction explains our canons.

3 Major Sources Employed

All studies of medieval English boroughs have emphasised the wide range of privileges possessed by places that were called 'boroughs', and one of the objects of Ballard & Tait's methodical tabulation of the content of individual charters was to demonstrate the width of that range. Once one has passed beyond charters as evidence of burghality there is a range of evidences no less wide and varied, any one of which, in our view, entitles a place to be reckoned a borough. Few places can claim every class of evidence, and some boroughs, usually the more petty, enter the *List* by passing one of our tests only. In drawing up the tests that would be used to admit places to our *List* we realised that at some point we should have to draw a line arbitrarily, and we are morally compelled to set out our tests not only for criticism but to enable those who would urge wider or narrower tests to know where they must prune and where augment our *List*.

In the first place we resisted the temptation to include a place simply because it is known to have had an urban character in the Middle Ages. 'Urban', on analysis, turns out to be an even more elusive concept than burghality, but despite the loss from the *List* of some places[13] that one of us has publicly characterised as 'towns', we have persevered in strictness. As Tait himself once observed,[14] the definition of a medieval borough is a tempting but daunting excursion that leads from Manchester straight into Ariadne's web. But he rightly emphasised that the common feature, indeed the lowest common denominator of boroughs large and small, early and late, corporate and incorporate, royal, seignorial, or ecclesiastical, was the possession of burgage tenure. Tenurial freedom was the freedom that town air conveyed, and in the pettiest borough that was the extent of the fresh air blowing into the villeins' world. Thus, a document referring to burgage tenure or to burgages admits a place to our *List*.

This free tenure, distinct from the mass of villein tenures, marked out the burgess from the non-burgess as the name *burgage* marked out his place of living and work from the tofts and crofts, the messuages and the curtilages, of unprivileged contemporaries. This legal distinction between burgage and non-burgage was the essential basis of economic self-improvement outside agricultural and village crafts. While in some cases the improvement and the progress to urbanisation was small (or even abortive), the grant of burgage tenure was the basis of the economic fortunes of the vast majority of English medieval towns. The connection between this legal status and economic advancement is well known; one of us has treated it more fully elsewhere,[15] and it need not be elaborated here. Our present purpose is not to provide a history of burghality but simply to emphasise its importance as a historical fact by quantifying its extent.

What words other than those of formal charters, already discussed, can be accepted as proof of this burghality, and in what sources have they been sought? The plainest evidence is a contemporary use of the word *burgus*.[16] Since there was virtually no topographical literature in the Middle Ages, one is unlikely to encounter direct statements of the form '. . . *burgus est*', although there are occasional narrative situations where a 'borough' is attacked, burned, or visited, especially in the pre-Conquest annals of the *Anglo-Saxon Chronicle* (the special problem of the Anglo-Saxon *burh* is discussed further below). Much more frequent among our sources is the use of *burgus*, *burgagium*, or *burgensis* in documents such as a reeve's account, a tax assessment, a rent roll, or an 'extent' (that is, a survey and valuation). On these occasions the writer of the document was emphasising that very difference between burghal and non-burghal with which our *List* is concerned. His purpose was not historical analysis but to direct attention to those assets that were non-manorial.

In the case of the reeves' accounts, the isolation of burghal revenue (whether under a bold rubric or simply in a separate sentence) probably arose from the different nature of the tenures and the tenements concerned, although the smaller the borough, the less particular the differentiation between manor and borough in the layout of items. A separate rubric also emphasised the usual situation where burghality was no original feature of the estate but an addition to it or a transformation of part of it—an important *incrementum*, in the language of manorial accounting. This process of addition is best seen in manors where accounts survive in annual series from the years when burghality was being conferred on villein communities or on newly recruited populations. The Winchester Pipe Rolls cannot be bettered as an example. At Michaelmas 1218 the reeve of *Clere* (that is Burghclere and Highclere, Hants) accounted for nothing beyond normal manorial revenues, but twelve months later the account roll had a bold heading *Novus Burgus*, followed by the names of the burgesses who had taken up sixty-seven burgage plots at 1s a year rent.[17]

The feudal extents, those *post mortem* being the most numerous, were designed to give the king, as superior lord, an accurate assessment of the value of an estate. If a borough lay on it, the burghal revenues (direct and indirect) were as relevant as the profits of agricultural operations or as the tolls from the manorial mill. From the later years of Henry III onwards these documents have survived almost complete. Assisted by the ultra-violet reader where the ink is faded, and by the existence of duplicates filed in the Exchequer, the inquisitions *post mortem* have been among our most profitable sources for previously unrecorded burghality. We have systematically worked through the text of the sixteen volumes of the printed *Calendar*, seeking for mention of 'borough' (for, although the placename indexes are excellent, the majority of volumes have no subject index).[18] Where the burghal entry is fully transcribed in the *Calendar*, we have given a reference solely to the printed source. Our reference is to the Public Record Office call number (see p 19) only when the document itself has fuller information. There are also a small number of 'borough' items which the compilers of the *Calendar* thought not important enough to indicate at all: we have encountered these in the course of examining extents for places already under suspicion from some other source, but we cannot claim to have searched all the 1,305 files in this class, making up some 4,000 separate documents, many of which comprise more than one membrane.

The much smaller class of *Ancient Extents*, which arose from the forfeiture of land, is much more accessible through its incorporation in the printed *List of Rentals and Surveys*.[19] This *List* is arranged topographically, so that, while it does not systematically indicate burghal entries, it makes for easy access whenever a place is suspect from another source. The wide chronological and geographical range of the other types of document comprised in the PRO class, 'Rentals and Surveys', gives this *List* great importance in enquiries such as our own.

Whereas the reeve making up his annual account and the escheator making up his *extent* were led to separate burghal and non-burghal items for their own convenience, there were others whose work made for a more public declaration of separation. Chief among these were the local assessors of lay taxation and the Exchequer officials concerned with accounting for the sums locally collected. It was necessary to differentiate the borough communities from the rest simply because the tax rate per shilling of taxable wealth was higher in boroughs than elsewhere. The final and permanent embodiment of this differentiation was the 'fifteenths and tenths' that made up the basis of lay taxation from 1334, the larger fraction being paid where the collectors identified a borough. Many years ago Willard drew attention to this category of 'taxation boroughs', also noting how assessors and collectors were not always of the same mind from one year to another, since some places, though a minority, appeared one year as a vill and another as a borough. Further confusion can arise when such a place happened to be a royal estate (ancient demesne), for the dwellers on ancient demesne were also regarded as liable to pay tax at the higher fraction. Willard noticed that the taxation boroughs included some whose burghality was hitherto unnoticed by historians who had depended, as we have shown, mainly on charter evidence. His survey unfortunately ended with the tax collection of 1332, but we have been able to amplify his list of taxation boroughs by a complete search in the records of the important tax of 1334, the last reassessment before this form of lay taxation became conventionalised.[20]

The *Nomina Villarum* of 1316, a list of communities made for the levying of foot soldiers, attempted a similar differentiation between borough and vill, but many petty boroughs were not shown as such.[21] Willard included the evidence from 1316 in his tables and we have authenticated pre-1334 taxation boroughs solely by the reference 'Willard' except where we have encountered evidence among the class E179 that was unknown to him.[22] The records of the collection of the Ninth in 1342 and the poll tax in 1377 have yielded no boroughs additional to those assessed in or before 1334.[23]

The greater fraction of wealth paid by boroughs was a recognition not only of their wealthiness but of the indebtedness of the traders and craftsmen within them to the Crown for providing order and good government. Boroughs often sought to be distinct from vills in the administration of justice. Royal officials had to make public differentiation between borough and non-borough with the development of itinerant justice, administered by justices periodically visiting the provinces in eyre. At these visitations local juries were sworn to try the issues at hand, and normally there was a separate jury for each subdivision of the county, be it hundred or wapentake, as well as for those districts (some large, some small) that were accepted as liberties or juridical islands within a county. Many of these liberties were ancient royal estates, and one of the counterparts for this privilege was, as we have already seen, a higher rate of property tax than in the county at large. The same principle is found in the treatment of what, in a term parallel to Willard's 'taxation boroughs' we can call 'juridical boroughs'. Generally the cases heard from these non-hundredal areas were recorded under a separate rubric on the Eyre Roll, *burgus de* ... or *de burgo de* ... and not infrequently the Roll is prefaced by a membrane listing the jurors who had been summoned to the eyre and arranged so that the burghal jurors were separately grouped. Certain counties are fortunate enough to have surviving Eyre Rolls from the very beginning of the thirteenth century,[24] contemporary with the first Charter Rolls and earlier than the first extents, and it will be seen from our frequent reference to the PRO class JI 1 that this source significantly augments our knowledge of boroughs.

The PRO collection of surviving medieval court rolls has not provided fruitful material for us, although it is not difficult of access via *List and Index VI*. The collection of reeves' and other officers' accounts[25] (*List and Index IV* and *VIII*), however, rivals in usefulness the records from the escheators' inquisitions *post mortem*. Although they relate mainly to the Crown's medieval demesnes, they are augmented by accounts for lands that came temporarily to the Crown's hands through such causes as minorities of wards, forfeiture by treasons, or vacant bishoprics (see also *List and Index XI* for analogous documents enrolled on the Pipe). Accounts in these series have systematic internal arrangement, so that the revenue items, where the burghal references are most likely to occur, can be quickly located within even a bulky roll. *Burgus* rubrics are quite usual, and since these accounts are more spaciously set on the parchment than the extents, it is not so exhausting for the eye to scan rolls that lack *burgus* rubrics in order to seek the telltale phrases *de burgo*, *de burgagio*, or *de burgensibus*.

If medieval boroughs impinge at all on the minds of modern historians, it is most probably with the prefix 'rotten'. Only a minority of our 609 medieval boroughs, in fact, sent members to Parliament, and of this minority only a few were to degenerate so thoroughly that their names became a monotonous part of the long public debate that preceded Parliamentary reform in 1832. We cannot disguise that Old Sarum and Grampound owed their franchise to their medieval burghality, but since Parliamentary representation has been studied for so long by historians, and since the writs of summons have been in print for more than 150 years, this category of documentation has produced no surprise entries to our *List*.

While not coinciding with each other, the three classes (parliamentary borough, taxation borough, and juridical borough) shared one characteristic: these boroughs were selected as élite by those who administered taxation, provincial justice, and the issue of Parliamentary writs. So many other places with burghal tenure were treated as vills by tax assessors and so many petty boroughs had no separate jury representation at the judicial eyre that there must have been conscious acts of inclusion and exclusion. Even within these three élite classes the tests applied by different selectors were clearly not the same, otherwise the members of the classes would correspond: nor were selectors consistent, otherwise boroughs would not appear and disappear between one tax list and another, between one eyre and another, and between one Parliament and the next.

Domesday Book uses the word 'borough' or 'port' (and their derivatives) on many occasions.[26] Discussion of the Domesday and pre-Domesday boroughs of our *List* has been deliberately postponed to this point. Even Domesday, from 1086, is separated by more than a century from the earliest of the main non-charter sources discussed above. Yet a place that was burghal in *Domesday Book* usually (though not always) possessed burghality in later centuries, and we may safely assume some continuity between the burghal institutions of 1086 and those made explicit in the charter material of the next two centuries. *Domesday Book* itself was not concerned to spell out the nature of burghal privileges. Its pages show as great a variety in the words indicating burghality as we have already found in later documents of other types: and, indeed, *Domesday Book* omits to use burghal language for some places that, on other evidence, must have then had burghality.

Charters delineating burghality are rare, even in the quarter-century following Domesday, so that it is not surprising to have so little Anglo-Saxon material of this type. Our boroughs with first dates in the Anglo-Saxon period rest therefore on other categories of evidence. We have risked regarding all *burhs* as worthy of inclusion, rather than undertake, in the present state of archaeological exploration, a separation of those *burhs* (if any) which were no more than temporary places of refuge in time of trouble. The *burhs* of the Burghal Hidage[27] and the *burhs* of the *Anglo-Saxon Chronicle*[28] find their place in our *List*, therefore, as well as small numbers of places where the indicative word is *port* or one of its compounds.

4 Extensions to the List

In the course of our work for this *List* and for other purposes over the last decade we have explored fairly thoroughly the sources so far discussed, although we should be the last to claim exhaustiveness, and we fully expect to learn that other scholars have noted other evidences in the PRO sources, as well as in local archives, where our own scrutiny has been only haphazard. Documents of the types discussed above—particularly manorial accounts and estate rentals—are not confined to the PRO, and we have tried to examine relevant sections of the British Museum's manuscript collection. Similar categories exist in varying bulk in virtually all the local private and public archives, and our two-man part-time search could not extend to a pilgrimage through all of these, although we have had occasion to make ourselves familiar with the situation in Cornwall, Devon, Gloucestershire, and Yorkshire. Even here, by the kindness of archivists, new documents have been brought to our attention. In 1968 we were bold enough to send an enquiry to all the English archives appearing in *Record Repositories in Great Britain*. The response was most generous. Virtually everyone replied, even those with no burghal records of any period. There is not space here to thank all those who replied, but where particularly novel information was received we have acknowledged it (p 11). As documents continue to flow in to local repositories and as cataloguing progresses, there will undoubtedly be further augmentation of our *List*. Indeed local records are the most promising single source for further augmentation, and we shall continue to be grateful for references supplied.

5 Arrangement of the List

Our boroughs have been arranged alphabetically within counties (as they were in 1971). London is placed before Middlesex and York before the remainder of the Yorkshire entries, which are grouped by Ridings. There is also a single alphabetical index, with the county indicated.

The date at the left hand of each entry indicates what we believe to be the earliest occasion of recorded burghality. It may well be that the relevant document permits only a range of years to be assigned, and we have employed the convention ×. Thus, the charter of Henry II to the men of Lydd, Kent, has not been more narrowly dated than 1154 × 1158. Query marks and *circa* are occasionally employed. Where the document cited is of a date subsequent to the grant of burghality, our main date is that of the grant, and the date of the document is given in brackets in the course of the reference. Thus the date of the document granting the liberties of Hastings to New Romney is 1205, but the grant of liberties took place, as the document states, in the time of Henry I, so that 1100 × 1135 appears in our left-hand column. Posthumous evidences of this type are not infrequent, for, as the habit of seeking confirmation of his predecessors' grants from a newly crowned king developed, an enrolment of the confirmation brought to the Charter Roll or Patent Roll a record of an original grant from years before the Rolls commenced or from years when the habit of central enrolment had not taken firm hold. Some difficulties in close dating are discussed later (p 37).

Our main references, to the right of the date, set out as concisely as possible the earliest evidence for burghality that we have encountered for each place. The relevant words *port, burgus, burgagium, burgensis,* etc, are given in their English form and context. For taxation, juridical, and Parliamentary boroughs the facts of taxation at the higher rate, of a separate eyre jury, or of a writ of summons are adduced. We have not provided the text of borough charters, for, as we have shown, the vast majority of these can be studied in Ballard, Ballard & Tait, or Weinbaum; page references to these three frequently cited works have been given. Our aim has been to guide the reader to the source of evidence, since we could not within the scope of a hand-list provide him with the original text of the evidence. Any serious student of a place's burghality would need to study the context of the evidence, even when it is brief; and in many cases the evidence lies within a document that is far from brief. Wherever possible we have taken the reader to a printed source where he can find the text of the relevant document or a discussion of it. In the printed source cited he will find the location of the original document, should he require to consult it, so that our

B

references to archival sources are, in general, limited to documents hitherto unnoticed in print.

On the extreme right of each entry there usually appear the letters *R*, *E*, or *S*, denoting the source of the original grant. These indicate whether we have a royal, ecclesiastical, or seignorial grant; occasionally more than one class of grantor was involved. Table 3 sets out the distribution of these classes. It will be seen that classification is possible for nearly 90 per cent of the boroughs in our *List* (541 out of 609) and that multiple grantors appear in only nineteen cases. It should be stressed that original, or earliest known, grants are analysed and subsequent changes of owner have not been followed through: thus the large number of royal boroughs in fifteenth-century Cornwall derived from privileges granted by earls of Cornwall before the union with the Crown.

In general our references are the minimal for supporting a claim for burghality and, where possible, to date the first appearance of that burghality. An occasional further comment will be found where the references raise serious difficulties. Since this is a hand-list to aid in the identification of boroughs, we have resisted the temptation to multiply our references or to provide a selection of miniature borough histories.

Still less is this *Hand-List* a general history of the origins of English medieval burghality. Much more work needs to be done before anyone could re-enter that field after Maitland and Tait, especially at the level of petty burghality. The remainder of this Introduction is confined to general issues that have arisen directly from our own much more narrowly conceived work. The next section exemplifies some of the difficulties that we encountered in our work of identification, and the three succeeding sections are in effect commentaries on the three tables (1, 3, 10) that review three matters central to each of our entries: the nature of the evidence for burghality, the date of the earliest evidence, and the type of founder.

6 Boroughs, Burgages and Markets

It cannot be too much emphasised that this type of search for evidence is limited by the vagaries and chances of documentary survival.

Medieval historians are unlikely to come suddenly on unexpected sources such as monuments and inscriptions recording some forgotten burghality. Borough historians are dependent upon the chance survival of parchment and paper, for field and archaeological investigation can do no more than suggest an agenda of enquiry.

We have in mind here the fact that the medieval burgage plot commonly took on a characteristic shape—long and narrow, with one short side abutting on the market place or another principal street of the borough. The grouping of these burgages together, with roughly similar lengths, made for a compact envelope, delimiting the borough territory even when—as in the majority of medieval English boroughs —there were neither walls nor other defences. These burgage-plot patterns are clearest where there has been little or no post-medieval expansion of settlement outside the old limits and no massive rebuilding on new alignments within it: the best examples are afforded by the small planted towns, and Beresford has published a number of characteristic plans.[29] Whenever such a pattern of plots is noticed, it should give rise to speculation, which is not the same thing as assertive proof.

It must be confessed that it was the casual observation of this pattern at Charmouth, Dorset, which led one of us to seek, and to find, documentary evidence for a former burghality, but we do not claim that these topographical indications are a universal pointer. The greatest chance of confusion is not with the generality of villages, where the tofts and crofts that made up the curtilages of houses lack the uniformity just described, but with that smaller number of medieval villages where regularity was imposed on or alongside an older and more jagged pattern through what seem to have been acts of internal reorganisation. These are only just beginning to be recognised,[30] and their medieval character is authenticated by similar regular croft shapes within villages sites now totally deserted.

This further line of enquiry apart, a study such as ours is necessarily document-bound. Since there is no law determining whether a document survives or is lost, there are bound to be accidentally determined differences between the quality of evidence available from place to place.

Not the least of the difficulties of identification arises from a certain contemporary hesitation about the right word to use to describe the smallest settlements that had developed (or were being given) opportunities for economic activities beyond agriculture. Beresford had already drawn attention to this confusion among even the sophisticated clerks who compiled the bishop of Winchester's Pipe Roll.[31] New Alresford, Hants, is a quite separate community from the village of Old Alresford, and in 1200 a chronicle described its creation. The bishop built a new market place, with a market hall and a communal oven. In that same year the bishop obtained a market charter and two years later another charter for an annual fair. In 1208–9 the rents from this quasi-urban development were still being entered on the Pipe Roll under the rubric of (Old) Alresford manor. But when he came to compile the roll at Michaelmas 1211, the scribe hesitated. On the eleventh membrane of the roll he made a heading *Forum de Alresford*, and under it entered the rent from forty-five houses, four of them just built. Later he changed his mind, crossed out all these entries and stitched a small piece of parchment to the ninth membrane. On it the same entries were made, but the heading was significantly different: it now read *de Burgo*, and in subsequent years a burghal rubric appeared in the normal course of the roll. A hesitation between the aptness of *Forum* or *Burgus* had been resolved.

At Oswestry, Shropshire, the charter of 1190 × 1200 refers to burgesses who had taken messuages 'for the improvement of the market'. More recently, in work unpublished as we write, Dr R. H. Britnell has illustrated the same grey area between market and borough communities in Essex.[32] It was to the 'tenants of the market' at Harlow that Abbot Hugh of Bury granted burgage tenure (1213 × 1229), yet Witham Newland (or Wulvesford), a Templar creation, had a market and quasi-burgage tenure for its settlers without an explicit use of a term for burghality in any extant document.[33]

Not all English markets were located in places that aspired to burgage tenure. The relative numbers may not be precisely determined yet, but the magnitudes are clear. In Essex Dr Britnell reckons seventy-five market centres, but our *List* claims evidence of burghality for no more than fifteen of these. For England as a whole Dr Britnell estimates 2,000 new market grants between 1199 and 1350. Our Table 1 shows 266 places first receiving burghality between 1200 and 1300, and if we added all the fourteenth-century grants to these—since most were made before 1350—we should still not exceed 370. Clearly not every market had burghality, although every borough had a market and many of them had fairs.

We have sometimes added grants of markets, or markets and fairs, to our references. We do not claim that a seigneur necessarily obtained a market charter at the same moment as he initiated burghality, but the borough is very unlikely to antedate the market franchise, and the date of the market charter usefully delimits the borough's date when other evidences are imprecise.

7 The Chronology of Boroughs

The English economy acquired its boroughs one by one—even the most enthusiastic promoters were not able to match the occasions in Wales and Gascony where Edward I founded several towns on the same day—and our concern has always been to offer a date for the first documented burghality as well as to offer proof of burghality. Yet the same imperfection of sources that leaves a place's burghality in different degrees of doubt and certainty will also contribute to further uncertainties about the date of first burghality. The dating uncertainties are indeed more numerous, for there are many documents which establish burghality beyond doubt that cannot themselves be precisely dated. Thus we know only the regnal year in which Hugh de Mortimer gave his charter to Burford, Shropshire, and Henry III's regnal years ran from 28 October of one year to 27 October of the next; some bishop's charters are datable only from the year of the episcopate, which was unlikely to have begun neatly on 1 January; some charters, both royal and private, lack a date in their text and may be datable only to a particular reign or to the years between a seigneur's succession to his lands and his inquisition *post mortem*. Most tantalising of all is the form of words used when Lostwithiel received its charter of liberties from Robert de Cardinan, Lord of Bodardell, c 1195. The charter explicitly states that Robert was granting his burgesses all the liberties that his ancestors had given them 'on the day that they founded

TABLE I

FIRST EVIDENCES, BY COUNTY AND PERIOD

County	Anglo-Saxon	Domesday	By 1200	1201–50	1251–1300	Undefined 13th c	14th c	15th c	Post-medieval references	Total
Beds	1		1	2	1			1		6
Berks	1	1	2½	6½	1		2			14
Bucks	1	1	1	6			1			10
Cambs	1				2					3
Cheshire		1		1	10½		2½			15
Cornwall		1	2½	9½	7		8		2	30
Cumberland	1			1	3		4			9
Derby	1		1	3	1					6
Devon	5	1	6	12½	14½	3	21	4	7	74
Dorset	4	1		3	6		1		2	17
Durham			7	3	1					11
Essex	2	1	2	3	2½		4½			15
Gloucs	2	2	6	6	7		5		1	29
Hants	3		5½	8½	2		1		2	22
Herefords	1	2		3	8		2			16
Herts	1	4	1	1	3		1			11
Hunts	1				1		6			8
Kent	3	6	1	3			1	2		16
Lancs		1	2½	5	7½		3		1	20
Leics	1		1		1					3
Lincs	2	3	3	1½	2½			1		13
London	1									1
Middlesex			1							1
Norfolk	2	1	1	2						6
Northants	2		3	1½	1½		1	1		10
Northumb			6½	7½			6		1	21
Notts	1	1			1					3
Oxon	1		2	5	1		1			10
Rutland					1					1
Salop	2		3	3	8		3	2	1	22
Somerset	7	3	5	6	3		7			31
Staffs	3	1	5	3	8	1	1			22
Suffolk	2	5		2	1			1		11
Surrey	2		1½	4½				1		9
Sussex	3	5	2	6						16
Warws	1		3	3	5		2	1		15
Westmorland			2	1						3
Wilts	5	5	3	5½	2½		3	2		26
Worcs	2	2		2½	1½		2	1		11
Yorks: York	1									1
ER		2	3	1	2		1			9
NR			8½	½	4		1			14
WR		2	4	2½	5½		4			18
Total	66	52	96½	135	126½	4	95	17	17	609

the town (*die qua villam fundaverunt*)'. Thus in 1195 men remembered an exact foundation day for Lostwithiel, but we remain ignorant of it— even of its decade—for Robert's charter fails to name his ancestor.

The impossibility of close dating for all our evidences makes it necessary for Table 1 to be constructed by very broad divisions of time. (Foundations overlapping period boundaries have been assigned half to each period.) The second column, 'Anglo-Saxon', is reserved for those known to have existed before the Norman Conquest; the third adds those places which first occur as boroughs in *Domesday Book*; the fourth brings in those with first evidences between *Domesday Book* and the beginning of the Charter Rolls in 1199. Since thirteenth-century documentation is more abundant, it is possible to make the next dividing points at 1250 and 1300, leaving only four places no more closely dated than 'thirteenth century'. The fourteenth-century dates lie mainly before the Black Death (1348-9). Less than 3 per cent of our boroughs have their first evidences from the fifteenth century, and the same proportion derive from post-medieval sources (although, as explained above, almost certainly of medieval origin).

If the column totals are added we can set out the stock of boroughs at different times in these terms:

TABLE 2

STOCK OF BOROUGHS AT DIFFERENT DATES

	Number	Percentage of eventual total
By 1066	66	11
By 1086	118	19
By 1200	214½	35
By 1250	349½	56
By 1300	480	80
By 1400	575	96
By 1500	592	98
Conjectured medieval	17	
Total	609	

The two halves of the thirteenth century stand out as the period of most active burghal creations, contributing 21 and 24 per cent of the final total. This is consonant with the results of other studies and with what is accepted about the expansion of all sectors of the economy in that century.[34] One-third of all the planted towns of England, for example, date from the same period (although not all were boroughs); so do more than half the boroughs of medieval Wales and two-thirds of the *bastides* of English Gascony.

How do different counties diverge from the 'typical' distribution? It is as follows:

Anglo-Saxon	Domesday	By 1200	1201–50	1251–1300	14th century	15th century
11%	8%	16%	21%	24%	16%	2%

In many counties the total number of boroughs concerned is too small for the divisions to be of any statistical significance, but eight many-boroughed counties display great divergence. Two, Dorset (21 per cent) and Somerset (24 per cent), have an abnormal proportion of early-evidenced boroughs from the Anglo-Saxon period, the counties of the *burhs*; Wiltshire has an abnormal proportion (20 per cent) of boroughs first recorded in *Domesday Book*; Yorkshire, NR, and Northumberland have a more than normal proportion of places first evidenced between *Domesday Book* and 1200, and the latter county also has an unusually large proportion of boroughs from the first half of the thirteenth century; and Herefordshire (50 per cent) and Cheshire (70 per cent) are the counties where, so far as evidences go, the key period was the second half of the thirteenth century.

Subsequent sections of this Introduction return to chronological differences between counties in considering the types of founder, and it concludes with a brief discussion of the possible bias that the accident of documentary survival introduces whenever these county differences are at issue.

8 The Founders of Boroughs

Table 3 extracts the evidence we have collected about the founders of boroughs. In 89 per cent of the 609 boroughs of our *List* we have been able to identify the founders sufficiently to group them under the three categories of royal, lay seignorial, and ecclesiastical. 'Royal' includes

TABLE 3

TYPE OF FOUNDER, BY COUNTY

County	Royal	Ecclesiastical	Lay seignorial	R/E	R/S	S/E	Unknown	Total
Beds	2	2	1	1				6
Berks	7	4	3					14
Bucks	2		7		1			10
Cambs	1		2					3
Cheshire	2	1	6		1		5	15
Cornwall	8	8	10		1		3	30
Cumberland	1	3	1				4	9
Derby	2		2				2	6
Devon	4	15	51	1			3	74
Dorset	9	5	2				1	17
Durham		9	2					11
Essex	4	4	5				2	15
Gloucs	5	8	14	1	1			29
Hants	9	7	5				1	22
Herefords	2	4	8				2	16
Herts	2	5	4					11
Hunts	4	2	2					8
Kent	6	3	1	3			3	16
Lancs	6	4	10					20
Leics			1		1		1	3
Lincs	6	3	3				1	13
London	1							1
Middlesex			1					1
Norfolk	3		2	1				6
Northants	3	3	3				1	10
Northumb	6	3	10				2	21
Notts	2		1					3
Oxon	3	4	2				1	10
Rutland	1							1
Salop	5	5	10				2	22
Somerset	9	11	10				1	31
Staffs	3	7	7			1	4	22
Suffolk	4	1	2				4	11
Surrey	4	1	2				2	9
Sussex	6	2	2		1		5	16
Warws	2	3	8				2	15
Westmorland	2		1					3
Wilts	15	5	6					26
Worcs	1	4	5	1				11
Yorks: York				1				1
ER	3	3	2				1	9
NR	4	3	5				2	14
WR	1	1	13				3	18
Total	160	143	232	9	6	1	58	609

queens and princes but not earls (or dukes) of Cornwall, Chester, and Lancaster before the union of these estates with the Crown. 'Ecclesiastical' takes in monastic houses as well as the estates of archbishops, bishops, and cathedral chapters.

Thus, of all our boroughs, about one-quarter were royal foundations, another quarter ecclesiastical, and just over one-third seignorial. A small group, 3 per cent of the whole, had joint founders. Since the royal and ecclesiastical boroughs are more likely to appear in surviving archives than those of petty seigneurs, one would expect that most of the sixty-eight boroughs of unknown parentage (making up 11 per cent of the whole) would also be seignorial, making this group up to nearly one-half of the total.

It will also be seen that there were considerable differences between counties. Again one must not make much of the counties where the total numbers were small, but the counties with a large number of boroughs did not all owe their fecundity to the same type of grantor. In Gloucestershire, Herefordshire, Lancashire, Warwickshire, and Yorkshire, NR, the seigneurs' boroughs were in very much the same proportion as in the country as a whole. It was only in Buckinghamshire, Devon, and Yorkshire, WR, that the seigneurs' proportion rose to two-thirds or more (Cambridgeshire, with its small total, is ignored here). The 'royal' counties, with significantly more than the national average of one-third, were Berkshire, Dorset, Huntingdonshire, and Lincolnshire, which had more than half their boroughs from the king. It is to Durham, the prince-bishop's palatinate, that one must go to find the greatest proportion of church boroughs, although not all of these were the prince-bishop's. Hertfordshire had half its boroughs in ecclesiastical hands.

Of the monastic boroughs none were Cistercian. The many and great Cistercian houses dissociated themselves from burghal promotion, extensive as their estates were. This detachment, already noted by Dr Donkin, derived not so much from their ideal of isolated communities as from the relatively isolated character not only of the monasteries themselves but also of much of the land that their benefactors had bestowed upon them, coming, as they did, late in the queue for seignorial charity.

Table 4 continues the chronology of boroughs by considering in addition the type of founder involved at each period, marrying the information in Tables 1 and 3. The numbers in each division of the county matrix in Table 4 now become generally small, and more may be gained by first studying the national position in Table 3. As in Table 1, foundations overlapping period boundaries have been assigned half to each period, and the nineteen cases of joint foundation have been assigned half to each class of founder. There remain seventy-one boroughs (12 per cent of the total) where evidences of foundation and founders are insufficient.

There is a clear pattern in Table 5. The royal boroughs came first, and even after twenty years of the Norman Conquest 72 per cent of all boroughs were still royal. Ecclesiastical founders accounted for rather more than half of the remaining stock in 1086 but by 1200 the seignorial drive was well under way. Although in absolute terms the number of ecclesiastical boroughs increased sixfold between 1086 and 1300, the lay seigneurs increased theirs twelvefold, and even by 1250 were responsible for over a third of all English boroughs; by the end of the Middle Ages the proportion had hardly changed. The tortoise had beaten both the hares.

9 Local Frequency

In 1967 one of us wrote of the other: 'The high score for boroughs in the two counties (Devon and Gloucestershire) that Professor H. P. R. Finberg has investigated may arouse suspicions that high scores elsewhere only await his coming.' The present partnership was not envisaged when those words were written, although it had been initiated by the time that *New Towns* was published. A rough enumeration of medieval towns had been attempted in *New Towns of the Middle Ages* in order to demonstrate the varying proportions displayed by the 'planted' and the 'organic' as one moved from county to county.[35] The enumeration was a rough one, relying mainly on printed sources, and drawing in places that were not burghal by the stricter tests of the present *List*; and, in order not to overplay the significance of the plantations, a fairly liberal interpretation was given to 'town' in count-

43

TABLE 4

TYPE OF FOUNDER, BY COUNTY AND PERIOD

County	Royal AS	Royal DB	Royal By 1200	Royal 1201 –50	Royal 1251– 1300	Royal Post- 1300	Ecclesiastical AS	Ecclesiastical DB	Ecclesiastical By 1200	Ecclesiastical 1201 –50	Ecclesiastical 1251– 1300	Ecclesiastical Post- 1300	Lay Seignorial AS	Lay Seignorial DB	Lay Seignorial By 1200	Lay Seignorial 1201 50–	Lay Seignorial 1251– 1300	Lay Seignorial Post- 1300	Unknown founder and period	Total
Beds	1			1½					1	1½								1		6
Berks	1	1	2	2		1				3		1			½	1½	1			14
Bucks	1			1½										1	1	4½		1		10
Cambs	1															2				3
Cheshire		½			1	1					1			½		1	5		5	15
Cornwall				4½	4			1		3½	½	2			2	2½	1	5	4	30
C'mb'land	1										1	2				1			4	9
Derby	1		1													1	1		2	6
Devon	5								1	3	4	5		1	5	16½	9½	15	9	74
Dorset	4	½		1	4			½		1	2	2				1		1		17
Durham									5½	2½					2		1			11
Essex	2	1	1	1					1	1	½	1½				1	2	2	1	15
Gloucs	2	1	1½	¼	¼	1			1½	1	3	3		1	3½	5¼	1¾	3		29
Hants	3		2	2	1	1				6	1				3½	½		1	1	22
Herefords	1			1							4			2		2	3	1	2	16
Herts	1	1						2			2	1		1	1	1	1			11
Hunts	1			1		2						2					1	1		8
Kent	1	3½			1	2	1	2½	1							1			3	16

Leics	½												½		1				1	3
Lincs	3	1	2					1	1		1			1		1	1		1	13
London																			1	1
Middlesex															1					1
Norfolk	2	1		½					1	½						1				6
Northants	2					1			3							½	1½	1	1	10
Northumb			3	4					1			2			2½	3½		3	2	21
Notts	1				1			1												3
Oxon	1			2					1	3					1			1	1	10
Rutland					1															1
Salop	2		2		1					2	2	1			1	1	5	3	2	22
Somerset	5	3				1	2		2	2		6			3	3	3		1	31
Staffs	2		1				1		2½	1	2	1		1	2	1	3½		4	22
Suffolk	1	2			1		1							2					4	11
Surrey	1		1	2						1					1	1			2	9
Sussex	3	2½	1					1½	1					1		1			5	16
Warws	1			1					1			1			2	2	4	1	2	15
W'morland			2													1				3
Wilts	5	4	1	1	1	2		1	1	3½	½				1	1	1	3		26
Worcs	½	1					1½	1		½	½	1				2	1	2		11
York: York	½						½													1
ER		1			1				1	1					2		1	1	1	9
NR			4						1		2				2½	½	1	1	2	14
WR			1									1		2	2	2½	4½	3	2	18
Total	56½	25	27½	28¼	17¼	13	7	11½	27½	38	29	33½	½	13½	40½	67¼	58¼	52	63	609

TABLE 5

STOCK OF BOROUGHS AT DIFFERENT DATES, BY FOUNDERS

	Number			Percentage of eventual stock of each class			Percentage of total stock at each date		
	Royal	Ecclesiastical	Lay seignorial	Royal	Ecclesiastical	Lay seignorial	Royal	Ecclesiastical	Lay seignorial
By 1066	55½	7	½	34	5	¼	88	11	1
By 1086	80½	18	14½	49	12		72	16	12
By 1200	107½	46	54	66	31	24	52	23	25
By 1250	135¾	83½	121¼	83	59	54	40	24	36
By 1300	153	112	178½	93	76	79	35	25	40
By 1500	164	146½	227½	100	100	100	31	27	42
Unknown		71							
Total		609							

ing up the organic places. The stricter test of this *List*, explicit documentary reference to burghality, has therefore excluded some towns from the 531 noted in 1967: Buckinghamshire has one fewer town in this *List* than in the 1967 Table, and Cornwall eight fewer. Nevertheless, as Table 1 shows, the English total is now 609.

For reasons to be discussed below (p 55) the researcher who pursues our subject through the counties of England finds himself unevenly supported by the labours of other scholars. Thus there are counties where it can be confidently hoped that only i's remain to be dotted and t's to be crossed; in some—fortunately a diminishing number—local historians have been only dimly aware of medieval urbanism, and we have no doubt that in time our *List* will be augmented. These reservations must be therefore borne in mind when interpreting Table 9. In one or two counties, notably Dr Palliser's Staffordshire and Dr Britnell's Essex, we were fortunate in being able to take advantage of researches that had progressed ahead of our own, and at greater depth. The counties where our more recent researches have been able to increase significantly the number of burghal claims are shown in Table 6.

TABLE 6

MAJOR REVISION IN NUMBERS SINCE 1967

	1967	*1971*
Cheshire	8	15
Essex	9	15
Gloucestershire	21	29
Herefordshire	11	16
Shropshire	17	22
Somerset	25	31
Staffordshire	13	22
Warwickshire	7	15
Wiltshire	15	26

The revision has improved the position of Somerset, Gloucestershire, Wiltshire, Shropshire, and Staffordshire in this burghal league table, but it still leaves Devon with more than twice the number of any other single county; and at the other end, Cambridgeshire, Leicestershire, Middlesex, Nottinghamshire, Rutland, and Westmorland have three boroughs or fewer to their names.

TABLE 7

COUNTIES WITH THE GREATEST NUMBER OF BOROUGHS

Devon	74
Somerset	31
Cornwall	30
Gloucestershire	29
Wiltshire	26
Hampshire	22
Shropshire	22
Staffordshire	22
Northumberland	21

The mention of Rutland and Middlesex draws immediate attention to the need to move from absolute numbers and make some allowance for the differing areas of English counties. Is Devon's predominance simply due to its acreage, since it is the largest single county in England if the three Ridings of Yorkshire are treated separately? Since medieval boroughs, even coastal ports, depended for their prosperity on their hinterland, the available area is not irrelevant in explaining their frequency.

In *New Towns* a comparison was made not only between the numbers of planted and organic towns but between the intensity of urbanisation in the various counties. The measure employed for this 'intensity' was simply the area of a county divided by the number of its towns, to give an average catchment area for each town. Since medieval towns were not evenly spaced on the ground, this measure is of use for only the broadest of purposes. One would indeed be self-hypnotised by figures if one strove to erect anything of an argument on the difference between the 121,000 acres per town in Cumberland and the 125,000 acres in Westmorland; but there is surely something to be learned about the heterogeneity of northern England in the early fourteenth century when it emerges that across the Pennines in Northumberland it was possible to sustain towns with average catchment areas of 64,000 acres, or approximately twice the density of Cumberland and Westmorland, and in the Midlands to have towns with an average catchment area four times that of the Lakes counties.

TABLE 8

COUNTIES WITH THE GREATEST DENSITY OF BOROUGHS

	acres
Devon	1 per 22,000
Gloucestershire	1 per 27,000
Cornwall	1 per 29,000
Huntingdonshire	1 per 29,000
Staffordshire	1 per 31,000
Berkshire	1 per 32,000
Somerset	1 per 33,000
Wiltshire	1 per 33,000
Herefordshire	1 per 34,000

Yet it is still Devon which emerges as the county with boroughs thickest upon the ground. The average catchment area of a Devon borough was 22,000 acres (34¼sq miles), compared with the national average of 51,000 acres: the nearest rivals were Gloucestershire with 27,000 acres, and Huntingdonshire and Cornwall, each with 29,000 acres.

With the three contiguous south-western counties doing so well, it is almost as if petty burghality were an infection spread by some traveller down what is now the A34, from Gloucester to Penzance, but other counties had scores almost as impressive. Dorset (36,000) and Wiltshire (34,000) can be considered runners-up, and they also lie in the south-west. Five West Midland counties make up another group: Staffordshire (31,000), Herefordshire (34,000), Warwickshire (37,000), Shropshire (39,000), and Worcestershire (40,000). But it cannot be all contiguity, for we have passed over Berkshire with its 32,000 acres and Huntingdonshire with its 29,000. And if contiguity and similar terrain were all, how would one explain Huntingdonshire's neighbour, Cambridgeshire, which had no more than a trio of boroughs and consequently a large average catchment area of 187,000 acres, next but one to the bottom of the league table, and far less encouraging to boroughs than Cumberland or Westmorland?

Which county in England made boroughs least welcome? Why, Norfolk, a prosperous, densely populated, old-settled, trade-oriented county with a borough occurring only per 217,000 acres, and so strikingly different from the other East Anglian counties, Suffolk and Essex, that lie in the middle of the range displayed in Table 9.

TABLE 9

NUMBER OF BOROUGHS AND COUNTY DENSITIES

County	No of boroughs	Thousand acres	Thousand acres per borough	County	No of boroughs	Thousand acres	Thousand acres per borough
Beds	6	300	50	Norfolk	6	1,300	217
Berks	14	450	32	Northants	10	630	63
Bucks	10	480	48	Northumb	21	1,280	61
Cambs	3	560	187	Notts	3	520	173
Cheshire	15	620	41	Oxon	10	470	47
Cornwall	30	870	29	Rutland	1	97	97
Cumberland	9	970	108	Salop	22	860	39
Derbyshire	6	640	107	Somerset	31	1,030	33
Devon	74	1,650	22	Staffs	22	690	31
Dorset	17	620	36	Suffolk	11	940	85
Durham	11	620	56	Surrey	9	450	50
Essex	15	960	64	Sussex	16	900	56
Gloucs	29	770	27	Warws	15	560	37
Hants	22	1,020	47	W'morland	3	500	167
Herefords	16	540	34	Wilts	26	860	33
Herts	11	400	36	Worcs	11	440	40
Hunts	8	230	29	Yorks: York	1		
Kent	16	970	61	ER	9	740	82
Lancs	20	1,030	52	NR	14	1,350	96
Leics	3	520	173	WR	18	1,610	89
Lincs	13	1,690	130				
London	1			Total	609	31,357	51
Middlesex	1	220	220				

An important consideration in all arguments from the numbers of boroughs in different localities must, of course, be their different sizes. If the numerous boroughs of the south-west were exceptionally small (by the available measurements of taxable wealth or taxed populations), then it would not be particularly remarkable that there should have been so many of them. A full discussion of this point must wait the anticipated publication by Dr R. E. Glasscock of the local tax assessments of 1334, and also the publication of the poll-tax data from 1377, of which only a small part is yet in print. Yet some rough calculations made in 1967 did allow for the factor of town size by giving double weighting to towns with between 1,000 and 1,999 taxpayers in 1377; a triple weight to those having between 2,000 and 3,999; and quadruple weighting for those with between 4,000 and 7,900. Even after these adjustments, Cornwall and Devon headed the density table, and no very different result arises if the calculation is restricted to boroughs.

The predominance of these two counties in terms of density is even more remarkable if the quality of their terrain is considered. If the prospects for a borough rested on the agricultural potential of its hinterland, then boroughs should have occurred most frequently in the most fertile counties. The connection must be eschewed. Table 9 shows the fertile counties in East Anglia and the Midlands in middling or low ranking, and Norfolk receives the booby prize. It is true that some allowance must be made for the fen acreage in Norfolk, but drained land supported thirteenth-century populations as dense as any in England, as Professor Hallam has shown. If we allow for the water-logged areas of Norfolk, how much more ought we to allow for the moors of Devon and Cornwall in measuring the south-western counties against the typical English county! Yet to do this would further increase their lead in terms of burghal density per effective acre.

There are obviously many correlations that need to be tested before the predominance of Devon and Cornwall can be satisfactorily explained: the different categories of seigneur concerned in different localities (Table 3); the different chronologies in different counties (Table 1); the prevalence of river- and sea-ports locally; and the centrality and accessibility of old-established towns as an impediment to further burghal innovation.

Dr Hatcher has recently shown that Cornwall was not an insignificant agricultural county at the period when borough promotion was most flourishing; his work also demonstrates the important role of the tin industry in the regional economy.[36] What the proliferation of petty boroughs in the south-west may show is an interlocking consequence of their terrain. For many reasons rural settlement came late, and boroughs came late with it; it also came to new areas, and

TABLE 10

NATURE OF SOURCES FOR FIRST EVIDENCES

County	A–S Chronicle	A–S charters	Domesday Book	Eyre jury	Charters	Hundred Rolls	Lay subsidy	C… Cl… Ro…
Beds	1			2				
Berks		1	2	6	1	1	1	1
Bucks	1		1	5				
Cambs	1					1		
Cheshire			1		7			
Cornwall			1	7	10		6	
Cumberland					4			
Derby	1				2			
Devon		3	1	5	5	4	1	
Dorset		4	1	3	6			
Durham				2	6			
Essex	2		1	2	1			3
Gloucs			2	1	5		1	
Hants		3		2	8			
Herefords			2	2	1			
Herts	1		4			1	1	
Hunts	1					1	6	
Kent			6	3	2			
Lancs			1		13			
Leics				1				
Lincs	2		3		1			
London		1						
Middlesex								
Norfolk	2		1		1			
Northants	2		1				1	
Northumb					5		1	
Notts	1		1		1			
Oxon		1		1	2		1	
Rutland								
Salop	1	1		1	6			
Somerset		5	3	5	5		2	
Staffs	2		1	1	6			
Suffolk		1	5	2	1			
Surrey		2		2	1			
Sussex		3	5	2	1			
Warws	1				4		2	
Westmorland					2			
Wilts	1	3	5	1	2	1		
Worcs			2	1	1			
Yorks: York								
ER			2		3		1	
NR					7			
WR			2		5			
Total	20	28	53	58	125	9	24	

al tent olls	Pipe Rolls	PRO C(other)	PRO DL	PRO E	PRO SC	BM	County and local archives	Unknown	Total
							3		6
	I								14
	I	I					I		10
							I		3
							7		15
		2					4		30
		I			I		3		9
	I						2		6
		II		I	I	8	32	I	74
		I					2		17
	I						2		11
		I					4		15
	I	5				I	II	2	29
							6	2	22
		4					6	I	16
		I		I				I	11
									8
							I	3	16
		2	I		I		2		20
							I	I	3
	I	I	I				4		13
									1
							I		1
							I	I	6
				I			5		10
	I	7					7		21
									3
	I						4		10
							I		1
		2				I	10		22
	2	2		I	I		3	2	31
							II	I	22
							2		11
	I						3		9
	I						I		16
		I		2		I	4		15
	I								3
			I		I		7	2	26
					I		5	I	11
								I	1
					I		2		9
							6		14
	2	I	I		4		3		18
	15	43	4	6	11	11	168	19	609

new boroughs appeared to service and further stimulate the colonisation; the economic base of this late settlement was diversified, and the boroughs profited from exchanging diversities; and difficult inland transport may have encouraged more frequent nodal resting places than in the English plains.

10 The Bias of Sources

Table 10 quantifies the source material available to us and described in section 3 above. It will be seen that the Charter Rolls are by far the most important single source for the earliest evidences of burghality. If all other documentation had perished, we should still know that just over one-fifth of the 609 places in our *List* were boroughs. Yet the Charter Rolls are a collection of documents rather than a single document: the primacy for a single source rests with *Domesday Book*, bringing in fifty-three boroughs to our *List* beyond those forty-eight that were already known from the *Anglo-Saxon Chronicle* or from pre-Domesday charters. Sources mentioned so far in this paragraph are accessible in print, but very few of the eyre jury-lists have been published, and the contribution of this source to our *List* is of the same magnitude as the *Domesday Book* contribution.

Since there are few Lay Subsidy Rolls before the late thirteenth century, they do not figure greatly in our Table, although we have frequently cited them as confirmatory evidence; and if the Table were not confined to first evidences, the *post mortem* inquisitions would also have shown up strongly.

As a group, documents in county and other local archives made an even more important contribution to our evidences than any source mentioned so far, making up 28 per cent of the total in Table 10, but this classification conceals not only a scattered location but also a heterogeneous character, being made up of charters, deeds, account rolls, etc, which, if they were in the central records, would have been assigned to their own columns.

One might have assumed that the quality of our knowledge of burghality in a particular county depends in some major way on the bulk of records surviving in local archives, and also on the bulk of material printed by the local Record Societies. But God has not been all on the side of the big archival battalions. The old-established Record Offices, for example, of Bedfordshire and Essex do not possess any more first evidences to people their counties with boroughs than the offices of a dozen other counties with newer and smaller repositories.

This is important in assessing the significance of the very different intensity of borough creation that one finds as one moves from county to county. Low scores for counties such as Bedford and Cambridge do seem to rest on genuine local differences of experience in the Middle Ages and not on the accessibility or the survival of records. The case of Bedfordshire also shows that even a long-established local Record Society cannot produce boroughs out of thin air.

In fact the counties where our searches have been most facilitated are those with a printed County History of the calibre of Hutchins's *Dorset* or the *Northumberland County History*, together with an archaeological society whose *Journal* and Record publications attain the standard of the Leicestershire and Staffordshire societies. The degree of interest displayed in boroughs by the *Victoria County History* is usually good, Hampshire and Herefordshire being the best of the prewar volumes. Warwickshire is a sad exception: although it has a separate index volume, *borough* is an entry that the compiler passed over, and even when the text mentions a borough (as at Southam), there is no cross-reference under the 'Southam' entry in the index.

Table 10 does more than demonstrate the relative importance of different sources for our knowledge of the fact and date of a place's burghality; it emphasises that if history is forced to rely on a small number of sources, there will be particular problems where those sources are defective.

Is there some relation between the existence of particular archival sources and the discovery of counties with an exceptionally large number of boroughs? It is true, as Table 10 shows, that Devon's high score rests, for example, on first evidences that were found in local sources, but the dominant rôle of the Duchy estates in Cornwall ensures that nine-tenths of the relevant records for that many-boroughed county are now located in London. Gloucestershire, with twenty-nine, and Somerset, with thirty-one, have about the same number of boroughs, but only three Somerset boroughs depend on locally sited evidences while the number for Gloucestershire is eleven. In Hampshire the bishops of Winchester's records increase the score of 'local archives' in the Table but the bishops' Pipe Rolls have spent more time on the road than most records. At different times they have been in Winchester, then with the Ecclesiastical Commissioners, then at the Public Record Office, and are now back in Winchester with the county archivist.

There does not seem to be any systematic bias within the source material to explain the exceptionally large number of boroughs evidenced in certain counties. What bias there is affects accuracy of dating rather than evidence for existence. A place of any size that was granted burghality after 1199 has a fair chance of being detected either in the Charter Rolls, the Pipe Rolls, or the Eyre Rolls; and if the foundation was after 1250, in the inquisitions *post mortem* or the Lay Subsidy Rolls. The very small boroughs of these periods are much more vulnerable to archival mischances. Boroughs of all sizes that were founded between *Domesday Book* and the first Charter Rolls (1199) are even more subject to the haphazard preservation of records. Here, the loss of Eyre Rolls for certain counties does import a potential bias. The incomplete national coverage of *Domesday Book* is the most serious loss of potential information. Had it included Durham, Northumberland, Cumberland, and Westmorland, we might have crucial evidence for the standing of Newcastle, Carlisle, and Durham in 1086 as well as for the forty-two other places in these counties that eventually received burghality. Similarly, the exempt jurisdictions of Durham and Chester excluded them from the ordinary process of medieval fiscal administration, and hence from appearing in sources central to our investigation; the palatinates' own surviving records do not make up the deficiency.

Yet there is a consolation. There were, after all, reasons for the omission of these northern Border counties from the Domesday survey and the erection of the privileged palatine jurisdictions—remoteness and insecurity. These conditions placed the areas beyond the direct control and scrutiny of London, and offered a poor soil for early burghal development other than as an appendage to a fortified centre; and whatever the Continental experience, the multiplication of small boroughs in England did not depend on walls and weapons. The four northern counties were not to be permanently barren of boroughs, as the forty-five entries in our *List* show.

11 *Envoi*

The survey of English burghality as revealed in our *List* is nearly ended. The number of boroughs has proved to be larger than we ourselves envisaged when we began to compile the *List*, and we know it cannot be complete. Yet, with its imperfections we believe that it shows energetic borough promotion concentrated in particular periods and in particular places; nor were the promoters the same types of men in all places and in all periods. The process of accumulation, our *List* confirms, was all but complete on the eve of the Black Death. If the promotion of boroughs arose from a realistic assessment of their chance of success in an expansionary economy, then the virtual end of promotion for more than a century must have its own significance, even after making allowance for the fact that towns had less attraction as refuges for villeins once villeindom in the countryside was in general decline.

The effective stock of English boroughs before the Black Death was made up, therefore, of no more than some 600 places. About a quarter of these were *de novo* plantations, and the remainder were existing places on which privileges were conferred. Working to augment this total is not the only way in which greater precision will be reached: some of our boroughs—perhaps no more than a handful—were abortive or very short-lived, and their number would have to be subtracted in order to arrive at the true total of pre-Plague boroughs. Yet if successful boroughs have so often failed to leave documentation for their birth day, it is not surprising that the death of the unsuccessful appears so rarely on the calendar of history.

M.W.B.

NOTES

1   For example, Stottesdon, Shropshire, with its first evidence the conveyance of a burgage in 1617. (Source references to this and other burghal evidence for particular places are not repeated in footnotes if they appear in the *List* itself)

2   G. H. Martin. Preface to Charles Gross, *A Bibliography of British Municipal History*, 2nd ed, 1966, i–xvi

3   A. Ballard. *British Borough Charters, 1042–1216,* 1913

4   A. Ballard & J. Tait. *British Borough Charters, 1216–1307,* 1923

5   M. Weinbaum. *British Borough Charters, 1307–1660,* 1943

6   T. D. Hardy. *Rotuli Chartarum in Turri Londinensi asservati, 1199–1216,* 1837

7   PRO. *Calendar of Charter Rolls, 1226–1257,* 1903

8   For example, seventeen of Ballard's charters were from this source

9   T. D. Hardy. *Rotuli Litterarum Patentium in Turri Londinensi asservati, 1201–1216,* 1835; and PRO. *Patent Rolls, 1216–1225,* 1901

10   J. H. Round, ed. *The Great Roll of the Pipe for AD 1186–1187,* Pipe Roll Soc, xxxvii, 1915

11   D. M. Stenton, ed. *The Great Roll of the Pipe for Michaelmas 1190,* Pipe Roll Soc, NS, I, 1925; the Pipe Rolls occasionally use the word *burgus* in recording tallage or aid payments; payment 'from the men' of a particular place also implies a collective community, perhaps a borough

12   *Regesta Regum Anglo-Normannorum, 1066–1154,* 4 vols, 1913–69

13 The omissions include Alnmouth, Brigg, New Eagle, Newmarket, and Wardour

14 J. Tait. *The Medieval English Borough*, 1936

15 M. W. Beresford, *New Towns of the Middle Ages* (1967), Chap 7

16 The element 'borough' and variants frequently appear in minor place-names, eg in Kent, without implying burghality

17 Hants Record Office, Pipe Roll no 159274 (1217–18) and 159275 (1218–19)

18 PRO. *Calendar of Inquisitions Post Mortem and other analogous documents*, I, 1904, in progress

19 PRO. *Lists and Indexes*, xxv, 1908

20 We have been able to consult Dr R. E. Glasscock's typescript lists continuing those in his unpublished thesis, 'The Distribution of Lay Wealth in SE England in the Early Fourteenth Century', London PhD thesis, 1963

21 The text of the *Nomina Villarum* is in PRO. *Feudal Aids*, 6 vols, 1899–1921

22 J. F. Willard. 'Taxation Boroughs and Parliamentary Boroughs', in J. G. Edwards, ed. *Historical Essays in Honour of James Tait*, 1933, 417–35

23 1342: G. Vanderzee, ed. *Nonarum Inquisitiones in Curia Scaccarii*, 1807; 1377: PRO, E 179. The collectors of these taxes were not faced with a different rate in borough and non-borough and therefore paid little attention to status. One poll tax receipt for Northampton calls it a *vill*: E 179/155/27

24 These are listed but without details in PRO. *Lists and Indexes*, IV, 1910

25 PRO call numbers SC 6 and DL 29

26 In the absence (1971) of an accessible modern text of *Domesday Book* we

have used Farley's edition of 1783 and Ellis's continuation of 1816, with pagination identical to the original manuscript. The burghal and urban elements in *Domesday Book* are conveniently brought together county by county in H. C. Darby et al. *Domesday Geography of England*, in progress

27 We have used the text in A. J. Robertson, ed. *Anglo-Saxon Charters*, 1939, 246–8. We have omitted the unidentified 'Sceaftsege' and 'Eorpeburnan': for these see N. Brooks. 'The Unidentified Forts of the Burghal Hidage', *Med Archaeol*, VIII, 1964, 74–90; see also under Tisbury in our *List*

28 For the Chronicle we have used Professor Whitelock's translation in *English Historical Documents, c 500–1042*, 1955, 135–235

29 M. W. Beresford, op cit, Figs 8 (Olney, Bucks), 10 (South Zeal, Devon), 13 (Newton Poppleford, Devon), 18 (Grampound, Cornwall), 26 (Henley in Arden, Warws), 27 (Penryn, Cornwall), 36 (Wulvesford or Witham Newland, Essex), and 37 (Leeds, Yorks, WR)

30 See J. G. Hurst. 'The Changing Village Plan' in M. W. Beresford & John G. Hurst, eds. *Deserted Medieval Villages*, 1971, 117–31 and Fig 25

31 M. W. Beresford, op cit; Hants Record Office, Pipe Roll no 159270B (1210–11)

32 R. H. Britnell. 'The Economic Significance of Market Towns in the Thirteenth and Fourteenth Centuries', unpublished paper read to the Economic History Society Conference, York, 1971 and communicated by the author; fifty-three of the seventy-five markets in Essex had charters granted between 1199 and 1350; see also M. W. Beresford, op cit, 436–7

33 J. L. Fisher. 'The Harlow Cartulary', *Trans Essex Arch Soc*, NS, XXII, 1940, 251, a reference due to Dr Britnell

34 See the data in H. Stoob. *Forschungen zum Städtewesen in Europa*, I, (Cologne 1970), 17, 19, 112 and 113; M. W. Beresford, op cit, Chaps 11–13

35 M. W. Beresford, op cit, 437 and Table IX. 10

36 J. Hatcher. *Rural Economy and Society in the Duchy of Cornwall, 1300–1500,* 1970, Chaps 1 and 8 and Appendix C for agricultural colonisation and tin-mining output

HAND-LIST OF ENGLISH MEDIEVAL BOROUGHS

Arranged by Counties

BEDFORDSHIRE

Bedford   R

915   Edward the Elder 'obtained the borough' of B[1]—
        Anglo-Saxon Chronicle[2]
1011   Capital of a shire—ibid
1086   Burgesses mentioned—DB, i, 209a, 218b; also the *prepositus* of the borough, 207c
1226   The burgesses stated that they had received charters
        from William I, William II, and Henry I, but that the
        charters were burnt in the siege of 1153—*Curia Regis
        Rolls*, XII, 513
1166   Charter of Henry II confirming to the burgesses all the
        liberties and free customs they had under Henry I—
        Ballard, 8

Biggleswade   E

1132   Manor granted to bishop of Lincoln—VCH *Beds*, II,
              212b
1199 × 1216   Market granted by King John; confirmed 1227—*Rot
              Chart*, 33
1247   Alienation of a burgage—*Beds Hist Rec Soc*, VI, 1919,
              135. Later there were 123 burgages rented at 1s each—
              J. Godber. *Hist of Beds*. 1969, 59

---

[1] In this and subsequent entries the name of the borough is abbreviated to its
initial letter when occurring within a reference.

[2] All our references to the *Anglo-Saxon Chronicle* are to the text translated by
Dorothy Whitelock. *English Historical Documents, c 500–1042*, 1955, *sub anno*.

Dunstable   E

c 1114   Town established by Henry I—Dugdale, *Monasticon*, VI,
              239
1131–2   Foundation of Augustinian priory, with grant of the
              manor, borough, market, school, vill, and all free
              customs—*Beds Hist Rec Soc*, X, 1926, 241
1179   First mention of *prepositus*—*VCH Beds*, III, 360

Leighton Buzzard   R–E

1086   Toll from the market—DB, I, 209*b*
1202   Represented as a vill by its own jury at the eyre—
              Beds Hist Rec Soc, I, 228, §225, and III, 141, §§341–9
1295   Taxed as a borough—Willard, 430

Luton   R

1086   Toll and market—DB, I, 209*b*
1202   Represented as a vill by its own jury at the eyre—PRO
              JI 1/1 m 5*d*
1221   Mentioned as a borough—*Beds Hist Rec Soc*, X, 1926,
              143

Toddington   S

1482   Rubrics in court roll refer to tenements in the borough
              and outside it—Beds Record Office, X 21/395

BERKSHIRE

Abingdon   E

1086   Ten traders dwelling in front of the church door pay
    40d—DB, I, 58c (S. V. Barton)
1225   Represented as a borough and vill by its own jury at
    the eyre—PRO JI 1/36 m 1d
    Portmote held by the abbot's bailiffs—*Cal Pat Rolls
    1292–1301*, 211; ibid, *1313–17*, 504–5
1327   Burgesses extort a charter (subsequently revoked) em-
    powering them to elect their own *prepositus* and bailiffs
    —*Cal Pat Rolls, 1327–30*, 211–22

Aldermaston   S

1299   Four tenants in burgage pay 8s 2½d—*Cal Close Rolls
    1296–1302*, 231
1432   Heading of court roll refers to the portmote—*VCH
    Berks*, III, 388

Bray   R

1225   Represented as a hundred, vill, and borough by its
    own jury at the eyre—PRO JI 1/36 m 4d

Cookham   R

1225   Represented as a hundred, vill, and borough by its
    own jury at the eyre—PRO JI 1/36 m 1d

Faringdon   E

1205   Manor granted to Beaulieu Abbey. In thirteenth cen-
    tury burgages, portmote, and bailiff mentioned—*VCH
    Berks*, IV, 492

1225   Represented as a hundred, manor, and borough by its own jury at the eyre—PRO JI 1/36 m 1*d*

Hungerford   R

c 1170   Charter under seal of the community of the burgesses of H—*Cartulary of St Frideswide*, Oxford Hist Soc, XXXI, 1896, 330

Lambourne   S

1225   Represented as a borough and vill by its own jury at the eyre—PRO JI 1/36 m 1*d*

Newbury   S

1189 × 1217   The borough of N was formerly held by the count of Perche (1189 × 1217)—*Rotuli Hundredorum*, I, 13

1225   Represented as a borough and vill by its own jury at the eyre—PRO JI 1/36 m 5

Old Windsor   R

1086   Ninety-five messuages in the vill—DB, I, 56*d*

1306   Taxed as a borough, but styled vill 1307–36—Willard, 430

Reading   R

1086   The King has in the borough of R twenty-eight messuages paying £4 3s—DB, I, 58*a*

Thatcham   E

1121   Granted to Reading Abbey

1306 onwards   Taxed as a borough (styled vill in 1307)—Willard, 430

1330–1424   Grants of burgages—S. Barfield. *Thatcham and its Manors*, 1901, 23, 26, 27, 39, 41

Wallingford   R

945   Grant of land at Brightwell, including several acres around the 'castellum' of W, and referring to W as a *port*—Birch. *Cart Sax*, no 810

1066–86   Long account of the borough—DB, I, 56a

1156   Charter of Henry II granting the most ample privileges to the burgesses in return for their great services in helping him to maintain his hereditary right—Ballard, 7, 13, 46, 80, 85, 94, 117, 123, 150, 153, 182, 204, 210, 238, 248

Wargrave   E

1189   Manor granted to the bishop of Winchester

1225   Represented as a hundred, vill, and borough by its own jury at the eyre—PRO JI 1/36 m 4*d*

Windsor   R

1131   A yardland described as 'capta ad burgum'—*Pipe Roll*, ed Hunter, 126

1225   Represented as a borough and vill by its own jury at the eyre—PRO JI 1/36 m 4*d*

1277   Charter of Edward I granting the burgesses of W a free borough with sundry privileges, including a merchant guild—Ballard & Tait, 3, 24, 79, 132, 239, 260, 282

BUCKINGHAMSHIRE

Amersham   S

1086 onwards	The manor held by the de Mandevilles
1227	Represented as a borough and vill by its own jury at the eyre—PRO JI 1/54 m 15
1307–22	Taxed as a borough; 1332–6 styled vill—Willard, 430

Aylesbury   R–S

1086	No mention of a market, but 'of toll, £10'—DB, I, 143*b*
1204	Manor granted by King John to Geoffrey, Earl of Essex
1227	Represented as a borough and vill by its own jury at the eyre—PRO JI 1/54 m 17
1307, 1322, 1332	Taxed at the urban rate as a borough; as a vill, 1315, 1316, 1319, 1334, 1336—Willard, 430

Brill   R

1227	Represented as a borough and vill by its own jury at the eyre—PRO JI 1/54 m 16
1294 onwards	Taxed at the urban rate: styled borough in 1316; in other years vill—Willard, 430

Buckingham   R

914	Edward the Elder stayed four weeks at B 'and made both the boroughs, on each side of the river'—*Anglo-Saxon Chronicle*
995	Charter of Ethelred II refers to 'my *prepositus*' in B—Kemble, *Codex Diplomaticus*, no 1289

1086	Twenty-six burgesses. 'Bishop Remigius holds the church of this borough'—DB, I, 143*a*
1227	Represented as a borough or vill by its own jury at the eyre—PRO JI 1/54 m 19

Fenny Stratford S

1204	Monday market granted to Roger de Caux
1253	Fair granted
1370	Extent mentions burgesses of a moiety of the town— PRO C135/216/11

Great Marlow S

1107 × 1121	Manor granted to earl of Gloucester
1183	Borough of M fined 5 marks—*Pipe Roll Soc*, XXXII, 1911, 81
1227	Represented as a borough and vill by its own jury at the eyre—JI 1/54 m 16
1307 onwards	Taxed as a borough; styled vill 1332, 1334, 1336— Willard, 430

Newport Pagnell S

1086	The burgesses have 6½ plough-teams—DB, I, 148*d*
c 1100	Manor acquired by the Paynel family
1227	Represented as a borough and vill by its own jury at the eyre—PRO JI 1/54 m 17*d*
c 1245	Fifty-three burgesses—*Cal Inq Misc*, I, 8

Olney S

c 1200	Manor granted to Ranulf, Earl of Chester
1227	Represented as a borough, vill, and manor by its own jury at the eyre—PRO JI 1/54 m 17*d*

Wendover   S

	A royal manor until 1151
1227	Represented as a borough and vill by its own jury at the eyre—PRO JI 1/54 m 17*d*
1307, 1315, 1322	Taxed at the urban rate as a borough; as a vill 1316, 1319, 1332, 1334, 1336—Willard, 430

Wycombe   S

| 1226 | Final concord between the burgesses of W and Alan Basset, settling their grievances against him, with his grant of the borough in fee-farm—Ballard & Tait, 11, 116, 128, 228, 277, 303 |
| 1237 | Confirmation of the foregoing by Henry III; similar confirmation by Edward I, 1285—ibid, 33 |

CAMBRIDGESHIRE

Cambridge   R

917	Headquarters of a Danish army—*Anglo-Saxon Chronicle*
1010	Head of a shire—ibid
1066	A borough with 373 messuages—DB, 1, 189*a*
1086	Twenty-nine burgesses—ibid
1120 × 1131	Charter of Henry I granting juridical and mercantile privileges—Ballard, 116, 168
1185	Charter of Henry II granting the burgesses their town in fee-farm—ibid, 221

Linton   S

| 1246 | Grant of market and fair to William de Say |
| 1279 | Forty-nine burgages—*Cambs Hist Jnl*, IV, 1933, 198 |

Swavesey   S

1279   A number of burgages held of Elena de la Zouche—
              Rotuli Hundredorum, II, 469*b*

CHESHIRE

Altrincham   S

c 1290   Charter of Hamon de Massey to the burgesses of A
              granting sundry privileges, including a portmoot and
              guild merchant—Ballard & Tait, 52, 60, 67, 81, 88,
              126 *bis*, 155, 211, 219, 266, 280, 356

Chester   R–S

1066   A city with 487 houses and a mint—DB, I, 262*b*
1086   Number of houses reduced to 282. Burgesses and four
              churches mentioned—ibid, 262*c*
c 1136   Stephen confirms customs of the borough as granted
              by William I and Earl Roger (d 1084)—*Regesta Regum
              Anglo-Normannorum*, III, no 181
1171, 1188–9 Royal charter—Ballard, 9, 81, 215
1190 × 1212   Charter of Ranulf de Blundeville, Earl of C, granting
              to his citizens of C their merchant guild—ibid, 206

Congleton   S

1272 × 1274   Charter of Henry de Lacey, Earl of Lincoln and Con-
              stable of Chester, granting a free borough to the bur-
              gesses of C with the right to elect a mayor, catchpoll,
              and ale-tasters—Ballard & Tait, 5, 49, 58, 79, 87, 125,
              153, 198, 209, 219, 266, 280, 364

Frodsham S

1209 × 1228 Charter of Ranulf de Blundeville, Earl of Chester, granting sundry privileges to the burgesses of F— Ballard, 44, 50, 56, 62, 82, 98, 121, 156, 194

Halton R

1351 × 1361 Henry, Duke of Lancaster, claims to hold the vill of H as a free borough, with market, fair, court, and other rights—Ormerod, *Cheshire*, I, 703

Knutsford S

c 1292 Charter of William de Tabley to the burgesses of K, granting to each a burgage of 2½ selions of land, with a portmoot and other privileges—Ballard & Tait, 52, 60, 67, 83, 88, 126, 155, 198, 218, 356

1294 William de Tabley makes an agreement with his overlord, Sir Richard Massey of Tatton, dividing the thirty-eight burgages in K between them—Ormerod, *Cheshire*, I, 489–90

Knutsford Booths S

1292 Burgesses of KB distinct from those of (Nether) Knutsford—Ormerod, *Cheshire*, I, 495

1403–4 A burgage in KB—ibid, I, 496

Macclesfield R

1261 Charter of Prince Edward creating a free borough at M, with merchant guild and other privileges—Ballard & Tait, 3, 47, 76, 87, 124, 153, 218, 266, 280, 354

Malpas (see also ADDENDA, p 193)

1288   Two burgages in M claimed—*Chetham Soc*, NS,
LXXXIV, 1925, 103, 121, 127

Middlewich

1288   Inquest of military service: the borough of M owes
twelve foot-soldiers—*Chetham Soc*, NS, LXXXIV, 1925,
111

1352   Charters of unspecified earls of Chester to M mentioned
at an enquiry—ibid, 22

Nantwich

1319–20 Borough mentioned in inquest—Ormerod, *Cheshire*,
1882, I, 426n

Northwich

1288   Inquest of military service: the borough of N owes
twelve foot-soldiers—*Chetham Soc*, NS, LXXXIV, 1925,
iii

Over   E

1280   Grant of a weekly market and yearly fair at O to Vale
Royal Abbey—*Cal Charter Rolls*, II, 237

ND   Charter by Walter Deaur, Abbot of Vale Royal,
creating a free borough at O—*Lancs & Cheshire Record
Soc*, LXVIII, 1914, 187–9

Stockport   S

c 1260   Charter of Robert de Stockport creating a free borough
at S with sundry privileges—Ballard & Tait, 3, 15, 55,
62, 63, 71, 86, 89, 91, 95, 100, 124, 145, 150, 194, 203,
208, 211, 221, 226, 229, 243, 263, 352

Tarporley   S

1281 × 1298   Grants of burgages on the terms laid down by Reginald
de Grey in his charter founding the borough—*Chetham
Soc*, NS, CVIII, 1944, xxvii–xxix, 298–300

CORNWALL

Bodmin   E

ND (eleventh   A woman sold at the church door in B; the portreeve
cent)   collects 4d in toll—J. Earle. *Hand-Book to the Land
Charters*, 1888, 273

1086   St Petroc has sixty-eight houses and a market here—
DB, IV, 183

1179   Townsmen fined 100s for setting up a guild without
licence

1201   Represented as a borough by its own jury at the eyre—
PRO JI 1/1171 m 3*d*

1227 × 1257   Charter of Richard, Earl of Cornwall, granting the
(?1229)   burgesses sundry privileges and exemptions—Ballard
& Tait, 117, 137, 232 *bis*, 265, 281, 290

Boscastle   S

1306 onwards   Taxed as a borough (in 1319 styled vill)—Willard, 430

Bossinney   R

1227 × 1256   Made a free borough by Richard, Earl of Cornwall—
Ballard & Tait, 5, 22, 132, 247, 250, 265

Camelford   R

?1257	Charter of Richard, King of the Romans and Earl of Cornwall, creating a free borough at C, with Friday market and yearly fair
1260	Confirmation of the foregoing by Henry III—Ballard & Tait, 4

Crafthole (in Sheviock)   S

1314	Weekly market and three-day fair granted to Nicholas Daunay, Lord of Sheviock
Sixteenth cent	Survey describes C as a borough—PRO LR 2/207. See also *Devon & Cornwall Notes & Queries*, XXIX, 293; Antony House MSS CM F2/159

Cuddenbeck

See St Germans (p 81)

Dunheved-by-Launceston   R

1086	A market (at St Stephen's) removed to D since 1066 by the count of Mortain—DB, IV, 188
1201	Represented as a borough by its own jury at the eyre—PRO JI 1/1171 m 3*d*
1227 × 1242	Made a free borough by Richard, Earl of Cornwall, with grant of land to the burgesses on which to build a guildhall—Ballard & Tait, 5, 111, 116, 132, 150, 239, 263, 311, 328, 343, 352, 370–1

East Looe   S

1154 × 1189	Market and fair granted by Henry II to Henry de Bodrugan
1284	Represented as a borough by its own jury at the eyre—PRO JI 1/113 m 12
1306 onwards	Taxed as a borough—Willard, 430

Fowey   E

1190 × 1225   Charter of Theobald, Prior of Tywardreath, establishing F as a free borough with sundry privileges—G. Oliver. *Monasticon Dioecesis Exoniensis*, 1846, 40. On the dates see H. R. Watkin. *History of Totnes Priory and Medieval Town*, 1914, II, 1016

1319   Styled vill, but taxed at borough rate; thereafter styled borough—Willard, 430

Grampound (in Creed and Probus)   R

1296 onwards   Taxed as a borough—Willard, 430

1297   Twenty-eight rent-paying burgesses—*Camden Soc*, 3rd ser, LXVII, 1945, 234

Helston   R

1086   The king has thirty villeins, forty *cervisarii*, twenty bordars, and twenty-three slaves in H—DB, IV, 92

1201   The men of H pay 40 marks of silver and a palfrey to King John that their town may be made a free borough with guild merchant—T. Madox. *History of the Exchequer*, 1711, 278. Charters of John establishing a free borough—Ballard, 3, 31, 110, 119, 189, 206, 228

Kilkhampton   S

1301   A market claimed by Richard de Grenville by prescription—*Placita de Quo Warranto*, 110

1306 onwards   Taxed at the urban rate: styled borough 1306, 1307, 1332, 1334, 1336; vill 1316—Willard, 430

Launceston   E

1086	A Domesday borough when deprived of its market
1141 × 1167	Charter of Reginald, Earl of Cornwall, to the canons and their burgesses (of St Stephen's), confirming all the liberties of a free borough which they retained when the count of Mortain transferred the Sunday market to Dunheved—Ballard & Tait, 379

Liskeard   R

1086	A market worth 4s—DB, IV, 207
1201	Represented as a borough by its own jury at the eyre— PRO JI 1/1171 m 3*d*
1240	Charter of Richard, Earl of Cornwall, creating a free borough at L with the same privileges as he had already granted to the burgesses of Helston and Launceston— Ballard & Tait, 5, 20, 104, 132

Lostwithiel   S

1194	Robert de Cardinan, Lord of Bodardell, pays 10 marks to have a market at L
ND	Charter of the same (c 1195) to his burgesses of L, granting them all the liberties which his ancestors had given them on the day when they founded the town— Ballard, 21, 41, 48, 66, 74, 76, 77, 119, 125, 154, 192, 217, 244
1268	Charter of Richard, Earl of Cornwall, amalgamating the boroughs of Penkneth and L with grant of market and fair, guild merchant, and other privileges—Ballard & Tait, 5, 147, 154, 227, 248, 250, 266

Marazion (alias St Michael's)   E

1085	Charter of Robert, Count of Mortain, granting to the monks of St Michael's Mount a Thursday market—Dugdale, *Monasticon*, VI, 989
1215	Burgesses of Marazion—*Devon & Cornwall Rec Soc*, NS, V, 1958, 46
1257 × 1272	Charter of Richard, King of the Romans, transferring three fairs and three markets, held by earlier royal grants on non-monastic land at M, to land of the priory—ibid
1306 onwards	Taxed as a borough—Willard, 430

Mitchell   S

1239	Grant to Walter de Ralegh, Lord of Degembris, of a weekly market and yearly fair at M
1284	Represented as a vill at the eyre by six jurors of its own —PRO JI 1/113 m 11*d*
1301	Styled borough at the eyre

Mousehole   S

	(Three miles south of Penzance, and like Penzance part of the manor of Alwarton)
1267	Grant of market and fair at Portheness—*Cal Charter Rolls*, II, 75
1327	Extent of Alwarton shows forty burgesses at M—*Cal Inq Post Mortem*, I, 24

Padstow (alias Aldestowe)   E

1306, 1307, 1313, 1322, 1332 1336	Taxed as a borough—Willard, 430

Penkneth (now Penknight)   S–R

1268   Charter of Richard, King of the Romans and Earl of
            Cornwall, to his burgesses of Lostwithiel and P (the
            western part of L), amalgamating the two boroughs
            into one—C. Henderson. *Essays in Cornish History*,
            1935, 46, 47

Penryn   E

1236   Charter of William Brewer, Bishop of Exeter, grant-
            ing free burgage to the burgesses of P—Ballard & Tait,
            46, 55, 95

Penzance   S

1327   Extent of Alwarton mentions twenty-nine burgesses
            in P—*Cal Inq Post Mortem*, I, 24 (see Mousehole, p
            80)

St Germans   E

1066   A Sunday market, ruined by 1086 because the count of
            Mortain had established a rival market (at Trematon)—
            DB, IV, 182

ND   The bishop of Exeter established a borough at Cudden-
            beck in this parish, with a portreeve elected by forty
            rent-payers. In 1562 it became the parliamentary
            borough of St Germans, and writs of summons were
            addressed to the portreeve—D. Gilbert. *Parochial Hist
            of Cornwall*, II, 1836, 63, 69

St Mawes   E

1306 onwards   Taxed as a borough—Willard, 430

Saltash (alias Ash)

1201 — Represented as a borough by its own jury at the eyre—
PRO JI 1/1171 m 3*d*

Tintagel R

ND (1227 × 1256) — Charter of Richard, Earl of Poitou and Cornwall, granting that the borough of T and its burgesses shall be free (confirmed 1386)—*Cal Pat Rolls, 1385–89,* 245

1306 onwards — Taxed as a borough—Willard, 430

Tregoney S

1201 — Represented as a borough by its own jury at the eyre—
PRO JI 1/1171 m 3

1306 onwards — Taxed as a borough—Willard, 430

Trematon R

1298 — Borough of T assessed separately from borough of Saltash—*Camden Soc,* 3rd ser, LXVIII, 1945, 237, 238

Truro S

c 1173 — Charter of Reginald, Earl of Cornwall, to his free burgesses of T, confirming privileges granted by Richard de Lucy (Lord of Lantyan, d 1179), and granting further liberties—Ballard, 17, 113, 117, 162, 191

Week St Mary

1306, 1307 — Taxed as a borough—Willard, 430

West Looe (alias Portbighan)   S

c 1243   Charter of Richard, Earl of Cornwall, granting to Odo
            de Treverbyn a free borough in his borough of 'Por-
            buan'—Ballard & Tait, 5, 137, 247, 249, 257, 290
1284   Represented as a borough by its own jury at the eyre—
            PRO JI 1/113 m 12*d*

CUMBERLAND

Carlisle   R

685   St Cuthbert shown round the city (the Roman Lugu-
            vallium) by Waga, its *prepositus*—*Two Lives of St
            Cuthbert*, ed Colgrave, 122
1130   The burgesses of C account for 100s from the silver
            mine—*VCH Cumb*, I, 338
1133   An episcopal see

Cockermouth

1260   178 burgages—PRO SC 11/730
1278   Represented as a vill by its own jury at the eyre—
            PRO JI 1/132 m 30*d*

Egremont   S

c 1202   Charter of Richard de Lacy creating a borough at E—
            Ballard, 21, 50, 56, 60, 67, 70, 73, 83, 84, 88, 90, 91,
            92, 93, 95 *bis*, 97, 105, 120, 139, 146, 148, 155, 159, 160,
            164, 193, 216, 249
1267   Grant of market and fair—*Cal Charter Rolls*, II, 75
1278   Represented as a borough and vill by its own jury at
            the eyre—PRO JI 1/132 m 28

Greystoke

1366 A borough—*Cal Inq Post Mortem*, XII, 35

Keswick

1373 Deeds, 29 Nov and 4 Dec, referring to two burgages in K 'in the vill of Castlerigg'—County Record Office, Carlisle

Newton Arlosh (alias Kirkby Johannis) E

1305 Charter of Edward I allowing the abbot of Holm Cultram to create a free borough at KJ in place of the one at Skinburness—Ballard & Tait, 7, 28, 133, 247, 249, 274, 367

Penrith

1286 Tenants in burgage mentioned—*Documents and Records illustrating the History of Scotland*, ed F. Palgrave, 1837, 5, 11

Skinburness E

1301 Charter of Edward I allowing the abbot of Holm Cultram to establish a free borough at S (cancelled four years later in favour of Newton Arlosh, qv)— Ballard & Tait, 6, 28, 133, 247, 249, 274, 366

Wavermouth E

1300 Charter of Edward I allowing the abbot of Holm Cultram to create a free borough at W (cancelled a year later in favour of Skinburness, qv)—*Cal Charter Rolls*, II, 488

DERBYSHIRE

Ashbourne

c 1200   Burgage mentioned—*Staffs Rec Soc*, IV, 1962, 120

Bakewell   S

1286   Charter of William Gernun conferring sundry privileges on his burgesses of B—Ballard & Tait, 17, 65, 81, 85, 87, 95, 125 *bis*, 167, 169, 180, 219, 223, 227, 233 *bis*, 267, 288, 298, 301, 340, 369

Castleton   R

1196   Four marks paid 'de cremento burgi de Alto Pech' (High Peak)—*Pipe Roll Soc*, NS, VII, 1930, 273

1255   43⅝ burgages—PRO SC 6 1094/11

Chesterfield   S

1204   Charter of King John for William Briwer, creating a free borough at C. Repeated 1213 for Richard Briwer and 1215 for William Briwer—Ballard, 3, 33, 35

Derby   R

917   The borough of D captured by Aethelflaed—*Anglo-Saxon Chronicle*

1048   A county town—ibid

1066   243 burgesses, 2 churches, 14 mills—DB, I, 280*b*

1086   100 burgesses, 40 lesser burgesses, 103 rent-paying dwellings, 10 mills, 4 churches—ibid

1204   Charter of King John confirming and extending the

privileges of the borough—Ballard, 8, 72, 104, 108, 164, 169 *bis*, 186, 199, 206, 229, 244, 248, 249

Wirksworth

c 1200   Burgage mentioned—*Staffs Rec Soc*, IV, 1962, 120

DEVON

Alphington   S

1304   Inquisition post mortem: extent includes rents from the borough of A, and from eight burgages—*Cal Inq Post Mortem*, IV, 152

Ashburton   E

Twelfth cent Market mentioned—F. C. Hingeston-Randolph, ed. *Register of Bishop Grandisson*, II, 1897, 1,570
1238   Represented as a borough by its own jury at the eyre—PRO JI 1/174 m 42d

Aveton Gifford   S

1384   Reference to a borough—BM Harl Ch 86/F/47
1429–1565   A number of references to burgage tenements—H. R. Moulton. *Palaeography, Genealogy, and Topography*, 1930, 187–92

Axminster   S

1209   Charter of King John for William Briwer, creating a free borough at A, with Sunday market and eight-day fair—G. Oliver. *Monasticon Dioecesis Exoniensis*, 1846, 360

Bampton S

1180 × 1210   Grant by Fulk Paynell to St Nicholas Priory, Exeter, of a free burgage in the borough of B—BM Cotton MS Vit D IX, f 157*b*

1302   Thirty burgesses—BM Harl MS 6126, f 62

Barnstaple R

c 1018   The borough court of B mentioned—*Crawford Charters*, 9

1086   Forty burgesses inside and nine outside the borough—DB, IV, 80

Bere Alston S

1295   Market and fair granted to the lord of Bere Ferrers—*Cal Charter Rolls*, II, 463

1305   Twenty burgesses paying rent of 1s each to the lord of Bere Ferrers—BM Harl MS 6126, f 68

Bideford S

1204 × 1217   Charter of Richard de Grenville creating a borough—Ballard, 32, 49, 62, 68, 76, 139, 143, 156, 194, 239, 245. Confirmed by his grandson—*EHR*, xv, 1900, 309

1238   Represented as a borough by six jurors at the eyre—PRO JI 1/174 m 36

Bovey Tracey S

ND (? early thirteenth cent)   Chartered by Henry de Tracey—BM Add MS 28649, f 218*d*

1326   Sixty-four burgesses—BM Harl MS 6126, f 111*b*

Bow (in Nymet Tracy) S

1259	Market and fair granted to Henry de Tracy of Nymet Tracy—*Cal Charter Rolls*, II, 19
1308	Inquisition post mortem: extent includes rent from the burgesses of *Nymetburghe*—PRO C134/10/12
1326	Four burgesses—BM Harl MS 6126, f 111

Bradninch S

1141 × 1157	Charter of Reginald, Earl of Cornwall, creating burgage tenure and other liberties—Ballard, 38, 46, 113, 243
1215 × 1220	Confirmation of the foregoing by Henry, son of Earl Reginald—ibid, 68, 76, 89, 157, 248
1238	Represented as a borough by its own jury at the eyre— PRO JI 1/174 m 29

Bridgetown Pomeroy S

1267	Grant to Henry de Pomerai of a three-day fair
ND	Charter of the same (1268) providing for an extension of the borough, which had been founded by his father—Ballard & Tait, 49, 58, 88, 96, 143, 179, 290
1293	Fifty-five burgesses—*Book of Fees*, II, 1,308

Chawleigh S

ND (c 1340)	Named as a borough—J. Brooking Rowe. *History of the Borough of Plympton Erle*, 1906, 13
1442	Inquisition post mortem on Hugh, Earl of Devon, refers to the borough of C—*Trans Devon Assoc*, XXXVIII, 1906, 335

Chillington   S

1309   Inquisition post mortem refers to an unspecified num-
              ber of burgesses belonging to the manor of Stoken-
              ham, and to the pleas and perquisites of the borough
              court—*Cal Inq Post Mortem*, v, 113

Chudleigh   E

1308   Described as a new borough—F. C. Hingeston-
              Randolph, ed. *Register of Walter de Stapeldon*, 1892, 24

Chulmleigh   S

1274   Eighty-three burgages held at a rent of 6d each—BM
              Harl MS 6126, f 20*b*

Colyford   S

1225 w 1238   Borough founded by Thomas Basset—*Rotuli Hun-
              dredorum*, I, 68
1238   Represented as a vill by six jurors at the eyre—PRO,
              JI 1/174 m 28
1274   112 burgages—BM Harl MS 6126, f 21
1340   Charter to the burgesses granted by Hugh de Courtenay,
              6 May 1340—Devon Record Office, 123M E77 (six-
              teenth-century copy)

Combe Martin   S

1249   Burgages mentioned—PRO JI 1/176 m 6
1326   Eighty-two burgesses—BM Harl MS 6126, f 113*b*

Crediton   E

1231 × 1242   Grant by William, Bishop of Exeter, to all the men of
              his borough of C—Exeter City Library, Pearse, Box
              33/1

1238   Represented as a borough by its own jury at the eyre—PRO JI 1/174 m 35*d*

1242   Described as a new borough—F. C. Hingeston-Randolph, ed. *Register of Bishop Bronescombe*, 1889, 5

?Cullompton

Described as *burgus* in 1640—Devon Record Office, 1508 M, surveys, VI

Dartmouth   S

1227   Grant of market and fair

1249   Amerced at the eyre for sending a jury of its own instead of coming with the Hundred of Coleridge as hitherto—PRO JI 1/176 m 34*d*

1341   Charter granting the right to elect a mayor, and other privileges—Weinbaum, 23

Denbury   E

1286   Weekly market and yearly fair in D granted to Tavistock Abbey—*Cal Charter Rolls*, II, 331

1393   Account rendered by the portreeve of the borough—Devon Record Office, 1258 W D5

Dodbrooke (in Kingsbridge)   E

1294–5   Grant of a tenement in Kingsbridge, mentioning the road leading to the new borough of D—Devon Record Office, 123 M/TB 93

1313   Taxed as a vill, thereafter as a borough—Willard, 431

1319   Borough said to exist here by royal charter—BM Harl MS 6126, f 101

East Teignmouth · E

1223	Dispute between William de Breuse and the canons of Exeter concerning a market in T—*Curia Regis Rolls*, XI, 126
1253	Market and fair granted to the dean and chapter of Exeter
1311	Grant of a house and two plots of land 'in the burgage of T'—Dean and Chapter Records, no 1809; ibid, no 1808, undated, may be a few years earlier: it refers to 'the borough of T St Michael'
1314–15	Rental of the borough—ibid, no 2946

Exeter · R

	One of the four *burhs* of Devon, with 734 hides assigned to it in the *Burghal Hidage*—A. J. Robertson. *Anglo-Saxon Charters*, 246
c 1018	The borough court of E mentioned—*Crawford Charters*, 9
1050	A cathedral city—Kemble, *Codex Diplomaticus*, no 791
1086	A city; 285 houses belonging to the king—DB, IV, 80

Great Torrington · S

?1135 × 1194?	Founded by William, third of that name, Baron of Torrington—J. J. Alexander & W. J. Hooper. *History of Great Torrington*, 1948, 9 and 70.
1238	Represented as a borough by its own jury at the eyre—PRO JI 1/174 m 34
1306 onwards	Taxed as a borough—Willard, 431

Harton (in Hartland) · S

1294 × 1299	Borough created by Oliver de Dynham—R. D. Chope. *The Book of Hartland*, 1940, 103

1299   Thirteen burgesses paying 1s each—*Trans Devon Assoc,*
        xxxiv, 1902, 425–8

Hatherleigh   E

1220   Thursday market and yearly fair at H granted to the
        abbot of Tavistock—PRO C60/12 m 2
1394   Burgage rents amounting to £6 19s 6d—Duke of Bed-
        ford's muniments, Devon Record Office, D5

Holsworthy   S

1309   Fifteen burgesses paying 1s each—BM Harl MS 6126,
        f 78b
1326   Nineteen burgesses—ibid, f 112b

Honiton   S

1193 × 1217   Borough founded by William de Vernon, 5th Earl of
               Devon—*Rotuli Hundredorum,* I, 74
1224   Burgage rents amounting to 13s 10½d—PRO E364/1
        m 3
1238   Represented as a borough at the eyre by twelve
        jurors—PRO JI 1/174 m 27

Ilfracombe   S

1249   Burgage tenements mentioned—*Devon Feet of Fines,* I,
        no 472
1326   Forty-nine burgages—BM Harl MS 6126, f 111b

Kennford   S

1300   Grant to Henry de Courtenay of a market and fair at
        K—*Cal Charter Rolls,* II, 488
c 1340 Named as a borough—J. Brooking Rowe. *History of
        the Borough of Plympton Erle,* 1906, 13

Kenton   S

1238	Represented as a vill by twelve jurors at the eyre—JI 1/174 m 41
1313	Taxed as a borough—Willard, 431

Kingsbridge   E

1220	Market granted to the abbot of Buckfast
1244	Represented at the eyre by six jurors of its own—PRO JI 1/175 m 43
1295–6	A rent of 12d per annum 'as by the other burgesses'— Devon County Record Office, 123M/TB93
1306 onwards	Taxed as a borough (styled vill in 1315, 1316)— Willard, 431

Little Totnes

1326	Fifty-eight tenants of Dartington were burgesses of 'Little Totnes'—*Cal Inq Post Mortem*, VI, 447–8

Lydford   R

	One of the four *burhs* of Devon, with 140 hides ascribed to it in the *Burghal Hidage*—Robertson. *Anglo-Saxon Charters*, 246
c 1018	The borough court of L mentioned—*Crawford Charters*, 9
1086	Twenty-eight burgesses inside and forty-one outside the borough—DB, IV, 80

Lympstone   S

1288	William de Albemarle draws 9s rent from burgesses of L—PRO C133/54/4

?Malborough   S

Described as a borough in surveys of 1640 and later—
Devon Record Office, 1508 M, surveys, VI

Modbury   S

1238   Represented as a borough at the eyre by twelve jurors
                of its own—PRO JI 1/174 m 39d
1306 onwards   Taxed as a borough (styled vill in 1313, 1316)—
                Willard, 431

Moretonhampstead   S

The will of Periam Pole, 1640, refers to 'the burrough
of Morton Hamsteed'—*Devon & Cornwall Notes &
Queries*, VII, 1912–13, 206. The Bowring Library, M,
contains a rental of the borough for 1799–1800, to be
collected by the portreeve

Newport (in Bishop's Tawton)   S

1291   Rental includes a *firma burgi*—PRO SC 6/1138/1
1308   Called a borough—F. C. Hingeston-Randolph, ed.
                Register of Walter de Stapeldon, 1892, 23

Newton Abbot   E

1269   Market and three-day fair granted to the abbot of
                Tor
1274–5   Described as 'nova villa', and a market grant of King
                John claimed—*Rotuli Hundredorum*, I, 72

Newton Bushel   S

1246   Tuesday market granted to Theobald de Englishville,
                life-tenant of the royal manor of Teignwick—*Cal
                Charter Rolls, 1226–57*, 311

| 1246 (six days later) | Licence to the same to assess burgages in the said manor and let them to whom he would—*Cal Pat Rolls, 1232–47*, 311 |

Newton Ferrers   S

| 1305 | Nine burgesses paying 1s each for their tenements—BM Harl MS 6126, f 68 |

Newton Poppleford   S

1226	Grant to William Briwer of a market at *Poplesford*—*Rot Lit Claus*, II, 132
1229	Grant to John Fitz Geoffrey of a four-day fair in his manor of Aylesbeare
1274	Borough of NP described as a member of Aylesbeare with 55½ burgages—*Cal Inq Post Mortem*, II, 50

North Ford   S

| 1326 | £11 17s 2d paid to William Fitz Martin in rents from sixty-eight burgesses 'at North Ford and elsewhere adjacent to his manor of Dartington'—PRO C134/99 |

North Molton   S

| 1249 | Represented at the eyre by its own jurors—PRO JI 1/176. (Styled a borough in the Lay Subsidy of 1524—PRO E 179/97/194) |

North Tawton   S

| | Still annually electing a portreeve in 1822—D. Lysons. *Devon*, 1822, 481 |

Noss Mayo   S

| 1286 | Grant of a market—BM Harl Ch 58 I 38 |
| 1309 | The borough 'called *la Nosse*'—PRO C134/16/9 |

Okehampton S

1086	The sheriff Baldwin has four burgesses in O and a market which pays 4s a year—DB, IV, 265
1194 × 1238	Charter of Robert de Courtenay for his burgesses of O—Ballard, 11, 48, 55, 67, 75, 77, 103, 119, 145, 154, 163, 178, 179, 193, 213, 239, 244, 248
1238	Represented at the eyre as a borough with twelve jurors of its own—PRO JI 1/174 m 41

Paignton E

1295	Weekly market and three-day fair at P granted to the bishop of Exeter (*A Survey of the Lands of William, 1st earl of Pembroke, 1567*, printed by the Roxburgh Club, 1909, II, 354–86, refers to 'free burgagers' and 'burgage lands' in P—cf *Trans Devon Assoc*, XVI, 1884, 703–24)

Pilton R–E

	'Pilton with Barnstaple' named as one of the four *burhs* of Devon, with 360 hides ascribed to it in the *Burghal Hidage*—Robertson, *Anglo-Saxon Charters*, 246. Superseded by Barnstaple (qv) before 1018
?1205 × 1222	Charter of Walter (?Loring), Abbot of Malmesbury, authorising the building of houses in P to be held in free and perpetual burgage at a yearly rent of 1s each— *Reg Malmesburiense*, Rolls Ser 72, II, 34

Plymouth

	See Sutton Prior
1439	Incorporated by Act of Parliament as the mayor and community of Plymouth—Weinbaum, 25; *Rot Parl*, V, 18–22

Plympton   S

	Foundation charter, c 1194, of William de Vernon, 5th Earl of Devon, produced in 1225—J. Brooking Rowe. *History of the Borough of Plympton Erle*, 1906, 80
1195	Burgesses mentioned—*Pipe Roll Soc*, XLIV, NS, VI, 131
1238	Represented as a borough by its own jury at the eyre— PRO JI 1/174 m 38d

Rackenford   S

| 1234 | Market and fair granted to Robert de Sydeham |
| 1448 onwards | References to the borough of R or Great Rackenford in Cruwys Morchard MSS: rolls of the borough court extant from 1515 |

Sampford Peverell   S

| 1300 | Twenty-eight free burgesses pay 28s 6d to Thomas Peverell—BM Harl MS 6126, f 57*b* |

Sheepwash   S

1230	Market and fair granted to Nicholas Avenel
1520	Inquisition post mortem on Nicholas Holand refers to the borough of S
1600	Burgage holders—PRO C2 Eliz, W12/35

Sidmouth   E

| Thirteenth cent | A borough with a portreeve—Lysons, *Devon*, 445, quoting the cartulary of Otterton |

Silverton   S

| 1321 | Forty free burgesses—BM Harl MS 6126, f 103 |

South Molton   S

1150 × 1170	Burgage tenure introduced by Gilbert de Turberville. Charter of confirmation, c 1199, by Payn de Turberville, printed *Trans Devon Assoc*, XXVI, 1894, 126
1238	Represented as a borough by its own jury at the eyre—PRO JI 1/174 m 32*d*

South Zeal   S

1299	Market and two fairs granted to Robert de Tony of South Tawton—*Cal Charter Rolls*, II, 479
1315	Twenty burgesses paying 35s 4d—*Cal Inq Post Mortem*, V, 400

Sutton Prior   E

1253	Market and fair granted to the prior of Plympton
1276	A borough—*Rotuli Hundredorum*, I, 95
1306 onwards	Taxed as a borough—Willard, 431
1439	Incorporated as 'Plymouth' (qv)

Tamerton Foliot   S

1298	Grant of a tenement in a borough of TF—Dean and Chapter MSS, Exeter, no 1796

Tavistock   E

c 1105	Market granted to the abbot of T—*EHR* LXII, 1947, 355
ND (c 1185)	Grant to the Hospitallers of a rent-charge from a burgage in T—H. P. R. Finberg. *West-Country Historical Studies*, 1969, 126
1220 × 1224	Borough court called the Shammel-Moot—ibid, 196, 197

1238   Represented as a borough at the eyre by a jury of its own—PRO JI 1/174 m 26

Tiverton   S

Possibly founded by William de Vernon, Earl of Devon, at the same time as Honiton and Plympton (qv)

1224   Burgage rents amounting to 25s 11½d—PRO E364/1 m 3

1238   Represented as a borough by its own jury at the eyre—PRO JI 1/174 m 29*d*

Topsham   S

1452   Extant account roll refers to a number of burgesses—Duke of Bedford's muniments, now in Devon Record Office

Totnes   R

c 1018   The borough court of T mentioned—*Crawford Charters*, 9

1086   Ninety-five burgesses inside the borough and fifteen outside—DB, IV, 313

1206   Charter of King John (spurious) creating T a free borough—Ballard, xxxviii, 3, 119, 122, 189, 206

1306 onwards   Taxed as a borough—Willard, 431

West Alvington   S

1272   Grant of weekly market and yearly fair

1304   Eight burgesses, each paying 2s 6d yearly, and one paying 4s—BM Harl MS 6126, f 65

West Teignmouth E

1292   A borough belonging to the bishop of Exeter—F. C. Hingeston-Randolph, ed. *Register of Bishop Bronescombe*, 1889, 473; cf *Rotuli Hundredorum*, I, 89, and *Trans Devon Assoc*, XXXVI, 1904, 106

Whitford (in Shute) S

1238   Represented as a borough and vill by its own jury at the eyre—PRO JI 1/174 m 28; see also m 26*d*

Winkleigh S

ND (1237 × 1251)   Grant of a burgage in W—Dean and Chapter MSS, Exeter, no 1941

1455   Deed referring to the portreeve of the borough of W—*Devon & Cornwall Notes & Queries*, 1919, 308–11

Wiscombe (in Southleigh) S

1248   Grant of a weekly market and yearly fair at 'the manor site of W'—Devon Record Office, 123 M/TB 433; see also *Cal Charter Rolls*, I, 331, sub 'Wiscum', not there identified

Late thirteenth cent   Grant of two burgages—ibid, 123 M/TB 436

1345   Grant of a burgage in W, lying between two other burgages—ibid, 123 M/TB 442

1365   Grant of ten burgages, four of which lay 'on the south part of the water of W'—ibid, 123 M/TB 444

1383   Grant of lands, rents, etc, in the manor and borough of W—ibid, 123 M/TB 445

Witheridge   S

1248	Market and fair granted to Roger Fitz Paine
1499	Named as a borough—*Trans Devon Assoc*, LXXX, 1948, 198

Woodbury   S

1286	Market and fair granted to William de Albemarle
1288	39s 7½d rent from burgesses—PRO C133/54/4

DORSET

Blandford   R

1244	Represented as a borough and hundred by its own jury at the eyre—PRO JI 1/201 m 7*d*
1272 × 1307	A free burgage—Hutchins, *Dorset*, III, 233
1306 onwards	Taxed at the urban rate; styled vill 1306, 1334, 1336; borough 1307, 1316, 1332—Willard, 431
1605	Incorporated—Weinbaum, 28

Bridport   R

An Anglo-Saxon *burh* named Brydian, with 760 hides assigned to it in the *Burghal Hidage*, may be either Bridport or Bredy—Robertson, *Anglo-Saxon Charters*, 246

1066	A borough and mint, with 120 houses—DB, I, 75
1086	100 houses in the borough—ibid
1244	Represented as a borough by its own jury at the eyre—PRO JI 1/201, m 5*d*

Castleton (in Sherborne)   E

1538   Court Roll refers to bailiffs of the borough of C—J. Fowler. *Mediaeval Sherborne*, 1951, 160

Charmouth   E

1320   Charter of William, Abbot of Ford, creating a free borough at C, with burgage plots 20 perches long and 4 perches wide, tenable by a yearly rent of 6d—Exeter City Archives, ED/M/300; G. Oliver. *Monasticon Dioecesis Exoniensis*, 1846, 352

Corfe   R

1268   Represented as a borough by its own jury at the eyre— PRO JI 1/202 m 23

1306 onwards   Taxed at the urban rate; styled vill 1306, 1316, 1322, 1334, 1366; borough 1307, 1313, 1315, 1319, 1332— Willard, 431

Dorchester   R

      The Roman *Durnovaria*, capital of the canton of the Durotriges

864   A Saxon royal residence—Birch, *Cart Sax*, no 510

1066   A borough with 172 houses and a mint—DB, I, 75

1086   88 houses standing—ibid

1106   Held in fee-farm by the burgesses—Hutchins, *Dorset*, II, 346

1244   Represented by its own burgesses at the eyre—PRO JI 1/201 m 6

Lyme Regis R

1284   Charter of Edward I creating a free borough at L, with merchant guild and other privileges—Ballard & Tait, 5, 25, 133, 283

1285   Charter of the same, confirming and amplifying the foregoing—ibid, 8, 105, 109, 110, 149, 185, 196, 199, 204, 212, 213, 214, 253, 254, 269, 276, 297, 302, 331

Melcombe R

1268   Represented as a borough by a jury of six at the eyre—PRO JI 1/202 m 24d

1280   Charter of Edward I conferring borough privileges—Ballard & Tait, 8, 24, 105, 109, 110, 149, 185, 196, 199, 204, 212, 213, 214, 253, 254, 269, 276, 297, 302, 331

Newton (in Purbeck) R

1286   Charter of Edward I creating a new town with the privileges of a borough—Ballard & Tait, 8, 105, 109, 110, 149, 185, 196, 199, 212, 213, 214, 253, 254, 269, 276, 297, 302, 331

1286   Another charter of Edward I, granting a market and fair—ibid, 247, 249

Poole S

c 1248   Charter of William de Longespée granting sundry privileges to the burgesses of P in return for a payment of 70 marks—Ballard & Tait, 16, 64, 74, 116, 197, 201, 271, 291, 339, 353, 369

1371   Charter of William de Montacute, Earl of Salisbury, confirming the foregoing and changing the title of portreeve to that of mayor—Weinbaum, 31

Shaftesbury R

An Anglo-Saxon *burh*, with 700 hides ascribed to it in
the *Burghal Hidage*—Robertson, *Anglo-Saxon Charters*,
247

1066   A borough with 257 houses—DB, I, 75
1086   177 houses standing—ibid
1244   Represented as a borough by its own jury at the eyre—
PRO JI 1/201 m 7d

Sherborne Newland E

1227–8   Charter of Richard, Bishop of Salisbury, for his free
men taking new burgages at Sherborne—Ballard &
Tait, 45, 54, 86

Stoborough S

A suburb of Wareham, called a borough in 1579—
Hutchins, *Dorset*, I, 99, but doubtful

Wareham R

An Anglo-Saxon *burh* to which 1,600 hides are assigned
in the *Burghal Hidage*—Robertson, *Anglo-Saxon Charters*, 246

1066   A borough with 285 houses—DB, I, 75
1086   135 houses standing—ibid
1244   Represented as a borough by its own jury at the eyre—
PRO JI 1/201 m 5d

Weymouth E

1248   Market granted—*Cal Charter Rolls*, I, 331
1252   Charter of the prior and convent of Winchester creating a free borough of W—Ballard & Tait, 4, 21, 47,
57, 87, 117, 142, 150, 211, 217, 222, 264, 290, 329, 353

Whitchurch Canonicorum   E

1265   Inquisition held in the borough of W—*Cal Inq Misc*, I, 199

Wimborne Minster   ?R ?E

1086   Burgesses mentioned—DB, I, 76

1362   Rents of assize of 77s 3d in the borough of W—*Cal Inq Post Mortem*, XI, 235

The town consists of two streets, East Borough and West Borough, probably separate boroughs—*Proc Dorset Nat Hist & Arch Soc*, LXXXIX, 1968, 168–70

DURHAM

Barnard Castle   S

c 1175   Charter of Bernard de Balliol confirming to the burgesses of BC all the free customs of the liberty of Richmond which they had by grant of his father—Ballard, 26

1215 × 1227   Confirmation of the foregoing by Hugh de Balliol—ibid

Bishop Auckland   E

1242–3   Represented by a borough jury at the eyre—JI 1/223 m 5

1308   Borough mentioned in account of temporalities—*Arch Ael*, 3rd ser, XII, 119; see also PRO SC 6/1144/17

Darlington   E

1183   A borough paying £5—DB, IV, 582b (Boldon Book)

Durham   E

1130
: Burgesses of D pardoned a fine of 100s because of the burning of their houses—*Magnus Rotulus Scaccarii*, ed Hunter, 1833, 132

1153 × 1181
: Charter of Bishop Hugh du Puiset granting to the burgesses of D all the free customs of Newcastle—Ballard, 25, 192

Durham (Old Borough) (alias Crossgate)   E

1229
: Agreement between bishop and convent—*Surtees Soc*, LVIII, 216

1242–3
: Represented by a separate jury from those of Durham, Elvet, and St Giles—PRO JI 1/223 mm 5, 5*d*
: The 'old' borough in contradistinction to the 'new' Elvet (qv)

Elvet   E

1188 × 1219
: Charter of Prior Bertram and his convent for the burgesses of their new borough of *Elvethalge*—Ballard, 41, 91, 97, 171

Gateshead   E

1153 × 1195
: Charter of Hugh du Puiset, Bishop of Durham, granting to his burgesses of G all the liberties of Newcastle—Ballard, 25, 53, 59, 81, 166

Hartlepool   S

1162 × 1185
: Charter of Adam de Brus granting to his burgesses of H the customs of Newcastle—Ballard, 251

1201
: Charter of King John granting that the men of H shall be free burgesses—ibid, 31, 101

c1380
: The burgages listed in *Sadberge* are probably those in

H—*Arch Ael*, 3rd ser, XII, 136, although a *Sadberge burgus* appears in 1235–6—JI 1/224 m 2*d*

Sadberge

See Hartlepool

St Giles   E

c 1180   Charter of Bishop Hugh du Puiset granting free bur-
              gage to the master and brethren of the hospital of
              Kepyer and their men—Dugdale, *Monasticon*, VI, 732

Stockton   E

1283   Borough mentioned; also in 1308, 1316—*Surtees Soc*,
              XXV, 1852, 383
c 1380   Thirty-nine burgages—*Surtees Soc*, XXXII, 1856, 164–
              70

Sunderland

See Wearmouth

Wearmouth   E

1180 × 1186   Charter of Hugh du Puiset, Bishop of Durham, grant-
              ing to his burgesses of W the customs of Newcastle—
              Ballard, 25, 54, 58, 64, 70, 71, 95, 96, 101, 103, 115, 116,
              133, 143, 146, 153, 158, 162, 168, 197, 214, 215, 218
1183   A borough paying 20s—DB, IV, 567*b* (Boldon Book)
              Later known as the borough of Sunderland (eg JI 1/223
              m 5, 1242–3)

ESSEX

Berden   E

1267	A fair granted to Berden priory—*Cal Charter Rolls*, II, 76
1369	A butcher is presented and amerced for dwelling outside the borough and selling against the assize—Essex RO, D/DU 565/2 m 17*v*

Chelmsford   E

1200	Charter to bishop of London that those taking up building plots on his demesne at C and at Braintree shall hold them with free customs pertaining—*Rot Chart*, 51*a*
1382	Bye-laws of the burgesses—Essex RO, D/DM M2 m 1, 1399

Colchester   R

A Belgic, Roman, and Danish town

917	'A great English host . . . went to Colchester and besieged the borough'—*Anglo-Saxon Chronicle*
1086	The king has 276 burgesses—DB, II, 104–7
1120 × 1130	Writ of Henry I to the burgesses of C—Ballard, 105
1189	Charter of Richard I conferring sundry franchises—ibid, 64, 82, 83, 84, 86, 119, 124, 133, 144, 147, 150, 151, 163, 180, 195, 201, 236, 242, 244
1227	Represented as a borough by its own jury at the eyre—PRO JI 1/229 m 17

Great Bardfield S

1253	Robert Maner, 'burgess of B'—*Cal Pat Rolls, 1247-58,* 199
1298	Rents of assize of borough given separately from those of manor—Essex RO, D/D Hu m 87
1329-30	Borough rents—PRO SC 11/799

Harlow E

1213 × 1229	Abbot Hugh grants burgage tenure to the tenants of the market 'as freely as our burgesses of St Edmunds and our other burgesses'—*Trans Essex Arch Soc,* NS, XII, 1940, 251

Harwich S

1222	Market granted to the earl of Norfolk—*Rot Lit Claus,* I, 523a
1274	William Fraunk, 'burgess of Harwich'—*Rotuli Hundredorum,* I, 140
1318	Borough charter—*Cal Pat Rolls, 1317-21,* 380

Hatfield Regis R

1198	Represented as a borough or vill by its own jury at the eyre—PRO KB26/9 m 8d

Maldon R

1086	The king has 180 houses held by burgesses—DB, II, 5b
1143 × 1147	Burgage mentioned—*Regesta Regum Anglo-Normannorum,* III, 201
1171	Charter of Henry II for the burgesses of M—Ballard, 39, 84, 90, 94, 123, 150, 185

Manningtree   E

1238   Grant of a market to Hubert de Roylly—*Cal Close
                Rolls, 1237–42*, 110
1286 × 1309   Referred to as a borough—*The Cartulary of Canonsleigh
                Abbey*, Devon & Cornwall Record Soc, NS, VIII, 1965,
                nos 229, 232, 234

Newport   S

1227   Represented as a borough or vill by its own jury at the
                eyre—PRO JI 1/229 m 15*d*
1272   Borough—PRO C132/42/1
1297   Rents received from plots in the borough—*Ministers'
                Accounts of the Earldom of Cornwall*, Camden Soc, I,
                1942, 48

Pleshey   S

1336   Burgesses and market stalls mentioned—PRO C135/
                48

Thaxted   S

1348   Rents of burgages listed—*Cal Close Rolls, 1346–49*,
                529, 533, 536, 539, 540
1483   Grant by Richard III to Cecily, Duchess of York, of
                the manor and borough of T for her life—Morant,
                Essex, II, 439

Waltham

c 1235   Half the tenants described in a survey as 'burgesses
                of the king's fee'—BM Cott MS Tib C ix, f 232, cited
                in *VCH, Essex*, V, 168

Witham   R

912   A *burh* built here by Edward the Elder—*Anglo-Saxon Chronicle*

Writtle

1382   Two butchers fined for dwelling outside the borough—Essex RO, D/DP M190

GLOUCESTERSHIRE

Berkeley   S

1190 × 1200   Grant of a burgage in B—I. H. Jeayes. *Catalogue of the Charters and Muniments at Berkeley Castle*, 1892, 24
1221   Represented as a borough by its own jury at the eyre—PRO JI 1/271 m 16
1235 × 1236   Grant by Thomas, Lord Berkeley, of sundry liberties to the burgesses of B—Ballard & Tait, 64, 73, 156

Bristol   R

1086   Burgesses mentioned—DB, 1, 163*b*
1188   Charter of John, Count of Mortain, granting sundry franchises to the burgesses of B—Ballard, 10, 40, 50, 77, 78, 82, 87, 96, 118, 133, 135, 139, 141, 143, 144, 147, 150, 152, 165, 184, 196, 206, 212, 216, 235, 237
1221   Represented as a borough by its own jury at the eyre—PRO JI 1/271 m 19*d*
1373   Created a county borough—*Bristol Charters, 1155-1373*, Bristol Record Soc, 1930, 118–41

Cheltenham E

1307   Taxed as a borough—Willard, 431
1333   Bailiff of borough makes presentments at the hundred
            court—PRO SC 2/175 no 25

Chipping Campden S

c 1180   Charter of Henry III (1249) ratifying creation of the
            borough by Hugh de Gondeville and Ranulf, Earl of
            Chester (1188–1232)—*Cal Charter Rolls, 1226–57*, 340

Chipping Sodbury S

1232   Grant by William Crassus of a burgage in his borough
            of S—*Cal Charter Rolls, 1226–57*, 173; cf *EHR*, xv,
            1900, 314

Cirencester R–E

1133   Foundation charter of C Abbey refers to burgesses—
            Dugdale, *Monasticon*, vi, 177
1169–99   Frequent references to borough and burgesses in taxa-
            tion accounts—*Pipe Roll Soc*, xiii, 114; xxvi, 46;
            xxxviii, 110; xxxix, ns, i, 55; xl, ns, ii, 95; xliv, ns,
            vi, 182; xlviii, ns, x, 31
1221   Represented as a borough by its own jury at the eyre—
            PRO JI 1/271 m 16
1343   Charter of Edward III granting that the abbey shall not
            in future be impeached touching any borough in C—
            Cal Charter Rolls, 1341–1417, 22, 23

Dursley S

1164 × 1189 Grant by Roger de Berkeley IV of a burgage in D—
            I. H. Jeayes. *Catalogue of the Charters at Berkeley Castle*,
            1892, 15
1287   Rent of freemen and burgesses—*Glos Inq pm*, iv, 142

Dymock   S–R

1216 × 1272	Undated extent mentions rent of 66 burgesses—*Glos Inq pm*, IV, 54
1288	A burgage abutting on the king's highway—BM Add MS 18461

Fairford   S

1221	Represented by its own jury at the eyre—PRO JI 1/271 m 13
c 1262	Borough mentioned—*Glos Inq pm*, IV, 33
1307, 1314	Sixty-eight burgesses pay 68s—ibid, V, 81, 143

Frampton   S

1308–9	Sir Robert fitz Payne proposed to make a free borough here—PRO C143/71/12

Gloucester   R

96 × 98	Founded as a Roman *colonia*
1007 × 1016	Head of a shire
1086	A city with an unspecified number of burgesses—DB, I, 162
1155	Charter of Henry II granting to his burgesses of G all the customs of London and Winchester—Ballard, 12
1483	Created a county borough—W. H. Stevenson, ed. *Records of the Corporation of G*, 1893, 16–19

King's Stanley   S

1295	Rents of the borough 50s 10d; profits of borough court 40d—*Glos Inq pm*, IV, 169

Lechlade S

c 1235
Charter referring to the new market and the inhabitants of burgages—C. D. Ross, ed. *Cartulary of Cirencester Abbey*, 1964, no 231

1246
Grant of an oven and two burgages—*Cal Charter Rolls, 1226–57*, 296

Marshfield E

1397
A messuage in the borough of M—*Glos Inq pm*, VI, 209

Minchinhampton E

1300
Three dwellings described as burgages—*Trans Bristol & Glos Arch Soc*, LIV, 1932, 315

Moreton-in-Marsh E

1273
Court called portmote, with an officer styled catchpole —*VCH Glos*, VI, 247

Fifteenth to sixteenth cents
Frequent references to burgage holders—ibid, VI, 245

Newent E

1298
Grant by the abbot of Cormeilles of a borough court, subject to a right of appeal to the court of the parent manor—BM Add MS 18461, f 74*b*

1313
Taxed as a borough—Willard, 431

Newnham R

1187
Borough of N pays 7s in the tallage of royal demesnes —*Pipe Roll Soc*, XXXVII, 142

1221   Represented by its own jury at the eyre—PRO JI 1/271 m 16

Northleach   E

c 1235   Charter refers to persons holding tenements other than burgages in N—*Hist et Cartularium Mon Gloucestriae,* ed W. H. Hunt (Rolls Ser, 1864–6), II, 36

ND   Grant by Henry, Abbot of Gloucester, of the moiety of a burgage 'in our borough of N'—ibid, II, 37

1266   Rents from 80 burgages—ibid, III, 176–78

Painswick   S

1324   Seven burgesses paying 13s per annum—*Glos Inq pm,* v, 186

1496   Rental referring to thirty burgages—W. St Clair Baddeley. *A Cotteswold Manor,* 1929, 120–4

Prestbury   E

c 1285   Thirty tenants holding each a burgage; other tenants dwelling in the borough—*Red Book of Hereford,* Camden 3rd ser, XLI, 1929, 25

St Briavels   R

1352   Grant to the burgesses of the town of St B that they shall be quit of toll and customs throughout the realm —*Cal Charter Rolls, 1341–1417,* 125

Stow-on-the-Wold   E

1107–8   Grant by Henry I to Evesham Abbey of a port and market at Eadwardestowe—*Cal Charter Rolls, 1226–57,* 258

1221   Represented by its own jury at the eyre—PRO JI 1/271 m 11

Tetbury S

ND   Charter of foundation by William de Braose (d 1211) granting all the liberties and free customs of the law of Breteuil—Glos RO, D 556/1-3

1287   Jury state that T is a borough—*Placita de Quo Warranto*, 259

Tewkesbury S

1086   Thirteen burgesses paying 20s a year—DB, I, 163c

1221   Represented as a borough by its own jury at the eyre— PRO JI 1/271 m 14d

Chartered by earls of Gloucester: Robert (1122–47), William (1153–83), Gilbert (1314)—*Cal Charter Rolls, 1327–41*, 424

Thornbury S

1243 × 1262   Foundation charter by Richard de Clare, Earl of Gloucester—*Gloucestershire Studies*, ed H. P. R. Finberg, 1957, 66

1296   Borough rents, £6 6s, court pleas 13s 4d; tolls 20s— *Glos Inq pm*, IV, 182

Wickwar S

1545   Earliest reference to borough—Glos RO, D 340

Winchcombe R

1007 × 1017   Capital of a shire amalgamated with Gloucestershire— T. Hearne, ed. *Hemingi Chartularium Eccl Wigorniensis*, 1723, 280

1086   A borough; twenty-nine burgesses enumerated—DB, I, 162c

1097 × 1101   Survey enumerating 151 burgesses—*Landboc Mon de Winchelcumba*, ed D. Royce, I, 1892, xiv

Wotton-under-Edge   S

1199 × 1216   Half a burgage in *Nocton* may refer to W—I. H. Jeayes. *Catalogue of the Charters and Muniments at Berkeley Castle*, 1892, 44 and 117

1253   Charter of Joan de Berkeley granting burgage plots, each of ⅓ acre, to be held for a rent of 1s a year, according to the custom of Tetbury—Ballard & Tait, 57, 62, 75

HAMPSHIRE

Alresford   E

1210–11   Styled borough for the first time in the Winchester episcopal accounts—Hants RO Eccles 2/159270 B, m 9, attachment

1236   Represented as a borough by its own jury at the eyre—PRO JI 1/775 m 19*d*

?Alton   R

1295   Parliamentary borough

Andover   R

1175   Charter of Henry II granting to the men of A a merchant guild and freedom of toll throughout the realm—Ballard, 185, 205

1205   Charter of King John granting to his burgesses of A the manor of A in fee-farm—ibid, 228

Basingstoke   R

1228	Charter of Henry III granting to the men of B the manor of B in fee-farm—Ballard & Tait, 307
1236	Represented as a borough by its own jury at the eyre—PRO JI 1/775 m 24*d*

Brading   R

1547	Grant to the bailiffs and burgesses of B of a market and two fairs—Weinbaum, 46. (See *VCH Hants*, v, 158. No medieval charter)

Fareham   E

1211–12	Increment in rental by three burgages—Hants RO Eccles 2/159271 m 4
1261	Grant of a burgage and stall in the borough of F—*Cal Pat Rolls, 1258–1266*, 158 (misprinted Farnham)
1284	Quitclaim by Edward I to the bishop of Winchester of all the king's right to F with the borough—*Cal Charter Rolls, 1257–1300*, 274

Lymington   S

1184 × 1216	Founded as a borough by William de Redvers, whose charter (not extant) was confirmed c 1256 by Baldwin de Redvers—*Cal Charter Rolls, 1226–57*, 470
1257	Grant to Baldwin de Redvers of a fair—ibid
1271	Charter of Isabella de Fortibus referring to an extension of the borough—PRO E142/85

Newport   S

1177 × 1184	Charter of Earl Richard II de Redvers for the burgesses of his new borough of Medina—Ballard, 252 its
1236	Called 'novus burgus de Insula', and represented by own jury at the eyre—PRO JI 1/775 m 23

Newtown (Burghclere)   E

1218	Grant of a fair at N—*Rot Lit Claus*, I, 1883, 363
1218–19	Account roll names fifty-two burgesses occupying sixty-seven plots in the new borough, paying 1s a year—Hants RO Eccles 2/159275 m 5d

Newtown (alias Fra(u)ncheville)   E

1254–5	House and land in new borough of Francheville—Hants RO Eccles 2/159296 m 5d
1256	Charter of Aymer, Bishop-elect of Winchester, granting to the burgesses of Frauncheville all the liberties of the burgesses of Taunton, Witney, Alresford, and Farnham—Ballard & Tait, 22

Overton   E

1217–18	Borough mentioned in the bishop's accounts—Hants RO Eccles 2/159274 m 5d and 10
1284	Quitclaim by Edward I to the bishop of Winchester of all the king's right to O with the borough—*Cal Charter Rolls, 1257–1300*, 274

Petersfield   S

1183 × 1197	Charter of Hawisa, Countess of Gloucester, confirmed 1198 by John, Count of Mortain, granting to the burgesses of P the customs of Winchester—Ballard, 27
1236	Represented as a borough by its own jury at the eyre—PRO JI 1/775 m 19d

Portchester   R

911 × 919	An Anglo-Saxon *burh* with 500 hides assigned to it in the *Burghal Hidage*—Robertson, *Anglo-Saxon Charters*, 246

1236	Represented as a borough by its own jury at the eyre—PRO JI 1/775 m 15
1258	Reference to the services of the burgesses—*Placitorum Abbreviatio,* 146

Portsmouth R

1106	Charter, said to have been given by Henry I to the men of P produced for inspection in 1686, now lost (ex inf M. J. W. Willis-Fear, City Archivist)
1194	Charter of Richard I, conferring on the burgesses of P a market, fair, and other privileges—Ballard, 29, 84, 123, 124, 151 *bis*, 171, 172, 187, 198

Romsey E

1236	Represented as a borough or vill by its own jury at the eyre—PRO JI 1/775 m 24

Southampton R

911 × 919	An Anglo-Saxon *burh* with 150 hides assigned to it in the *Burghal Hidage*—Robertson, *Anglo-Saxon Charters,* 246
962	Grant to Abingdon Abbey of the king's rent at S, and reference to Portmonna-hythe—Birch, *Cart Sax,* no 1094
1066	Seventy-six men on the king's demesne
1086	Sixty-five Frenchmen and thirty-one Englishmen, paying between them £4 os od—DB, I, 52a
1189	Charter of Richard I granting to the burgesses of S quittance of toll and all other dues—Ballard, 186

Stockbridge R

1236	Represented as a borough or vill by its own jury at the eyre—PRO JI 1/775 m 24

1233 × 1237   Burgages mentioned—L. C. Loyd & D. M. Stenton, eds. *Sir Christopher Hatton's Book of Seals*, 1950, 325

Twineham (Christchurch)   S

1315   *Inspeximus* of charters of Baldwin, Earl of Exeter, and of Baldwin, son of Baldwin, Earl of Devon—*Cal Pat Rolls, 1313–17*, 219

Whitchurch   E

1247 × 1249   Charter of John, Prior of Winchester, creating a free borough at W—A. W. Goodman. *Chartulary of Winchester Cathedral*, 1927, no 472

Wickham

1544   Borough distinguished from manor in survey—Hants RO 5 M50/1875

Winchester   R

     A Belgic and Roman city, *Venta Belgarum*
662   Seat of the West Saxon bishopric
911 × 919   A *burh* with 2,400 hides assigned to it in the *Burghal Hidage*—Robertson, *Anglo-Saxon Charters*, 246
1086   Scattered references to the city in DB
1155 × 1158   Charter of Henry II ratifying the customs of W—Ballard, 5, 80, 83, 98, 181, 197
1236   Represented as a city by its own jury at the eyre—PRO JI 1/775 m 20

Yarmouth   S

c 1170   Charter of Baldwin de Redvers granting the customs of free burgesses to his faithful men of Y—Ballard, 254
1236   Represented as a borough and vill by its own jury at the eyre—PRO JI 1/775 m 23

HEREFORDSHIRE

Bromyard   E

1250 × 1288   Value of the borough of B, £23 1s 6½d—*Red Book of Hereford*, Camden Soc, 3rd ser, XLI, 1929, 12

Clifford   S

1086   Sixteen burgesses—DB, I, 183*b*

Ewias Harold   S

1300   A number of burgages mentioned in inquest on John de Tregoz—A. T. Bannister. *History of Ewias Harold*, 1902, 117–20; PRO C133/94/9

Hereford   R

An episcopal see from 688

1066   The king has 103 burgesses, Harold 27, the bishop 98—DB, I, 179*a*, 181*c*, 182*d*

1189   Grant of fee-farm to citizens—Ballard, 222

1215   Charter of King John granting to the burgesses of H sake and soke, a merchant guild, and other privileges—ibid, 105, 114, 121, 189, 207, 209, 222, 238

Huntington   S

1267   Rent of burgages—PRO C132/34/8

Kington   S

1267   New Kington distinguished from borough of K—PRO C134/34/8

Ledbury   E

1250 × 1288   Total value of the borough £27 10s 7½d—*Red Book of Hereford*, Camden Soc, 3rd ser, XLI, 1929, 17

Leominster   R

1221   Represented as a borough, liberty, and vill by its own jury at the eyre—PRO JI 1/300d m 6

Longtown (or Ewias Lacy)   S

c 1234   Burgage mentioned—Duncumb. *Herefordshire*, II, 282
1271   Tolls of the borough—PRO C132/39/20
1310   100 burgages—PRO C134/14/19

Pembridge   S

1240   Charter of Henry of Pembridge to his burgesses of P—Herefords RO
1334   Rents and tolls from the borough—PRO SC 6 1209/4

Ploughfield (in Preston on Wye)   E

1273   41s 6d rents from borough—Hereford Cathedral, Chapter Estates compotus

Richard's Castle   S

1304   103 burgages—PRO C133/113/2

Ross-on-Wye   E

1250 × 1288   Total value of the borough £10 15s—*Red Book of Hereford*, Camden Soc, 3rd ser, XLI, 1929, 9

Stapleton S

1304   Thirty-four burgesses in S and the hamlet of *Froggestrete*
—PRO C133/113/2

Weobley

1255   Represented as a borough or manor by its own jury at
the eyre—PRO JI 1/300c m 23
1295   Parliamentary borough
1315 onwards   Taxed as a borough—Willard, 432

Wigmore S

1086   The borough there renders £7—DB, I, 183*c*

HERTFORDSHIRE

Ashwell E

1086   Toll and other dues of the borough bring in 49s 4d.
Fourteen burgesses—DB, I, 135*c*

Baldock S

1138 × 1185   A borough founded by the Knights Templar
1205 × 1219   Confirmation charter by William Marshall, Earl of
Pembroke—Dugdale, *Monasticon*, VI, 820

Berkhamsted R

1086   'In the suburb of this vill fifty-two burgesses pay £4
in toll and have half a hide'—DB, I, 136*b*
1255   Represented as a borough by its own jury at the eyre—
PRO JI 1/1/320 m 32*d*

Bishop's Stortford   E

1306–36	Taxed as a borough—Willard, 432
1311	Parliamentary borough
1345	Burgage rents, 5s 4d—PRO SC 6 1140/10

Hertford   R

912	'About Martinmas King Edward ordered the northern borough to be built, between the Mimram, the Beane, and the Lea'—*Anglo-Saxon Chronicle*
1011	A county town—ibid
1066	146 burgesses—DB, I, 132*a*

Hitchin   E

1268	Borough farmed for 8½ marks—PRO C 132/36/5
1470–1	Portman court—PRO SC 2/177/40

St Albans   E

1086	Forty-six burgesses hold ½ hide—DB, I, 135*c*
1248	Represented as a borough by its own jury at the eyre—PRO JI 1/318 m 26*d*

Standon   S

1262	A borough governed by a reeve—*Rotuli Hundredorum*, I, 188, 191 (Late seventeenth-century court rolls regularly mention a 'manor of the borough of S')

Stansted Abbots   S

1086	Seven burgesses besides the agricultural population—DB, I, 138*c* (? burgesses of Hertford)

Ware   S

1204   Robert Earl of Leicester's grant of free burgages at 2s
            pa in Inspeximus of 1447—*Cal Pat Rolls, 1446–52,* 51

Watford   E

1290   Taxed as a borough—PRO E179/120/2

HUNTINGDONSHIRE

?Alconbury Weston   S

1319   Taxed at the urban rate as a borough; in other years
            as a vill—Willard, 432

?Brampton   R

1319   Taxed at the urban rate as a borough; in other years
            as a vill—Willard, 432

Godmanchester   R

1212   Charter of King John granting the manor of G to his
            men of G in fee-farm—*Rot Chart,* 186
1319   Taxed at the urban rate as a borough; in other years
            as a vill—Willard, 432

?Hartford   E

1319   Taxed at the urban rate as a borough; in other years as
            a vill—Willard, 432

Holme   S

1279	Eight burgesses, forty-two cottagers, five free tenants—*Rotuli Hundredorum*, II, 652
1350	Sixteen burgages—PRO SC 6/876 16

Huntingdon   R

917	A *burh* captured by Edward the Elder—*Anglo-Saxon Chronicle*
1011	A county town—ibid
1086	A borough with 256 burgesses, 100 bordars, and 3 fishermen—DB, I, 203a
1100 × 1124	Charter of Henry I referring to the community and gelds of the borough of H—Ballard, 105, 107

?King's Ripton   R

1319	Taxed at the urban rate as a borough; in other years as a vill—Willard, 432

?Offord Cluny   B

1319	Taxed at the urban rate as a borough; in other years as a vill—Willard, 432
	The boroughs queried may simply be ancient **demesne**, taxed at the higher rate

KENT

Brasted

1227   Represented as a borough and vill by its own jury at
the eyre—PRO JI 1/358 m 18

Canterbury   R

The Roman *Durovernum Cantiacorum*

597   A seat of Kentish royalty and of an archbishopric

1086   A city in which the king had sake and soke over 212
burgesses and rent from 51 others—DB, I, 2a

1294 onwards   Taxed as a city—Willard, 432

Dover   R

1086   A Domesday vill with a guildhall, an unspecified number of burgesses, and special responsibilities for guard-
ing the coast—DB, I, 1a

1154 × 1189   Charter of Henry II granting the townsmen sake and
soke—Ballard, 114, 183; confirmed 1201 and 1205,
ibid

Faversham   R

1042 × 1066   Charter of Edward I ratifying the customs of F from
the time of Edward the Confessor—Ballard & Tait, 10,
41, 98, 115, 129, 148, 164, 165, 166, 178, 186, 188, 199,
260, 275, 331

1252   Charter of Henry III to his barons of F, granting sake
and soke and other privileges—ibid, 129, 147, 164, 199,
259

Fordwich
R–E

1086	A 'small borough' with seventy-three *masurae*; also six burgesses and seven *masurae*—DB, I, 12*b*
1070 × 1086	Charters of Odo, Bishop of Bayeux, and William I, granting F to St Augustine's, Canterbury—Ballard, 232

Hythe
R

1086	Six burgesses in Lyminge and 225 in Saltwood belong to the borough of H—DB, I, 4*a*, 4*c*
1156	Charter of Henry II, confirmed 1205 by John, ratifying all the customs of H from the time of Edward the Confessor—Ballard, 114, 123, 136, 182

Lydd
E

1154 × 1158	Charter of Henry II extending the privileges of the Cinque Ports to the archbishop's men of Lydd and Dengemarsh—Ballard, 184, 190

Maidstone

1474	A portmote and portreeve mentioned—K. S. Martin. *Records of M*, 1926, 1
1549	Incorporated—Weinbaum, 62

Newenden

1227	Represented as a hundred, borough, or vill by its own jury at the eyre—PRO JI 1/358 m 21

Queenborough
R

1368	Charter of Edward III granting the status of a borough to Q, with the right to elect a mayor and two bailiffs—*Cal Charter Rolls*, v, 221, 243

E

Rochester E

	The Roman *Durobrivae*
604	A cathedral city
1086	A city—DB, I, 8c
1227	Charter of Henry III granting to his citizens of R a merchant guild, the fee-farm of the city, and other privileges—Ballard & Tait, 105, 108, 110, 156, 184, 196, 204, 214, 255, 269, 278, 305
1446	Incorporated—Weinbaum, 64

Romney R-E

1086	A borough with eighty-five burgesses belonging to the manor of Aldington, twenty-one to Langport, and fifty to the hundred of Langport—DB, I, 4a, 4c, 10d
1100 × 1134	Charter of Henry II (1154 × 1189) confirmed 1205 by John, granting to the men of R all the liberties of Hastings as in the time of Henry I—Ballard, 9, 183

Sandwich R-E

1086	A borough with the same character as Dover—DB, I, 3a
1070 × 1086	Charters of Odo, Bishop of Bayeux, and William I, granting S to Christ Church, Canterbury—Ballard, 232, 233

Seasalter E

1086	Described as a small borough belonging to the archbishop's kitchen; no burgesses recorded—DB, I, 5a
1315, 1332	Taxed as a borough; 1307, 1313, 1334, 1336 as a vill—Willard, 432

Tenterden R

1449 Incorporated—*Cal Pat Rolls, 1446–52,* 276

Tonbridge S

1241 Represented as a borough and vill by its own jury at the eyre—PRO JI 1/359 m 37*d*

LANCASHIRE

Bolton S

1253 Charter of William de Ferrers, Earl of Derby, constituting B a free borough, with detailed specification of privileges—Ballard & Tait, 3, 15, 55, 62, 63, 64, 71, 86, 89, 91, 95, 100, 123, 128, 145, 150, 194, 204, 208, 211, 221, 226, 229, 243, 263, 352

Chorley S

1250 Acquired by William de Ferrers, Earl of Derby
1257 Burgages mentioned—PRO SC 6 1094/11

Clitheroe S

1258 Sixty-six burgages—PRO C132/21/13
1272 × 1291 Charter of Henry, Earl of Lincoln, granting to the burgesses of C all the liberties and free customs of Chester, which they had under his predecessor Henry de Lacy—Ballard & Tait, 29, 51, 67, 120, 224, 271, 320; see also p 335

Dalton   E

1239   Grant to Furness Abbey of a yearly fair at D; mention
        of a burgage—*Coucher Book of Furness Abbey*, Chetham
        Soc, 1886, 26, 27
1306   Taxed (for the only time) as a borough—Willard, 432

Flookburgh   E

1509   Burgages mentioned—DL 43/4/9

Hornby   S

1285   Burgesses mentioned in inquisition *post mortem*—*Cal
        Inq Post Mortem*, II, 341
1319   47½ burgages—ibid, VI, 102

Kirkham   E

1296   Charter of Walter, Abbot of Vale Royal, citing a char-
        ter of King Edward empowering him to have a free
        borough in the manor of K—Ballard & Tait, 2, 6, 60,
        84, 133, 170, 223, 283, 356

Lancaster   R

1193   Charter of John, Count of Mortain, granting to his
        burgesses of L the customs of Bristol—Ballard, 27, 55,
        59, 95, 97
1199   Charter of King John, substituting the customs of
        Northampton—ibid
1246   Represented as a borough or vill by its own jury at
        the eyre—PRO JI 1/404 m 25

Liverpool   R

1207   Charter of John granting to any who wish to take
           burgages at L all the liberties enjoyed by any free
           borough on the coast—Ballard, 32

1306   Taxed as a vill, thereafter as a borough—Willard, 432

Manchester   S

1301   Charter of Thomas Grelby for his burgesses of M,
           granting sundry privileges—Ballard & Tait, 17, 55, 71,
           86, 89, 91, 95, 100, 124, 128, 145, 150, 189, 194, 202,
           203, 208, 211, 212, 220, 221, 226, 235, 253, 263, 276,
           352, 370

Ormskirk   E

1286   Charter of the prior and canons of Burscough granting
           to the burgesses of O a free borough, with a portman-
           moot and other privileges—Ballard & Tait, 5, 51, 59,
           87, 126, 135, 146

Penwortham   R

1086   Six burgesses—DB, 1, 270a

Preston   R

1179   Charter of Henry II granting to his burgesses of P all
           the liberties of Newcastle-under-Lyme—Ballard, 27

Roby   S

1372   Charter of Sir Thomas de Lathom making his vill of
           R a free borough—Weinbaum, 67

Salford

c 1230   Charter of Ranulf, Earl of Chester, constituting S a free borough—J. Tait. *Medieval Manchester*, 1904, 62–111

Ulverston   S

c 1200   Gilbert, son of Roger, son of Reinfrid, grants a borough charter—Ballard & Tait, 380

1284   Charter of Roger de Lancaster exempting all the burgesses in his borough of U from all charges except those which pertain to their burgages and which are borne by the burgesses of Kirkby in Kendal—Ballard & Tait, 130

Warrington   S

1292   Borough created by William le Botiller

1300   Charter of the free tenants and community of W surrendering to William le Botiller, grandson of the founder, the court of burgesses with all its appurtenances—Ballard & Tait, 182, and cf 383

Warton   S

1246 × 1271   Charter of Walter de Lindsay granting to his free burgesses of W burgage tenure and other privileges—Ballard & Tait, 23, 49, 62, 64, 79, 113, 119, 125, 130, 177, 180, 191, 218, 301, 331

West Derby   R

1346 $31\frac{1}{2} + 1\frac{1}{2}$ burgesses—BM Add MS 32103, printed in *Lancs and Chesh Rec Soc*, LXX, 1915, 78–83

Wigan R

1246   Charter of Henry III creating W a free borough—
     Ballard & Tait, 3, 147, 164, 256, 272, 278, 284

LEICESTERSHIRE

Hinckley

1284   Represented as a vill by its own jury at the eyre—
     PRO JI 1/463 m 16

1295 onwards   Taxed as a borough—Willard, 432

Leicester R–S

     The Roman *Ratae Coritanorum*

679   Seat of a bishopric

1086   A city, with 320 houses, 65 burgesses, and 6 churches—
     DB, I, 230*a*

Mountsorrel S

1148 × 1153   Agreements between the earls of Chester and Leicester
     refer to the castle and borough of M—F. M. Stenton.
     The First Century of English Feudalism, 1932, 248–55
     and 285

1255   Burgage tenements in the fees of the two earls—PRO
     C132/17/9

1313   Taxed as a vill; as a borough 1315 onwards—Willard,
     432

LINCOLNSHIRE

Barton-on-Humber   S

1086	A market and tolls—DB, I, 354*c*
1216 × 1272	Portmoot recorded—R. Brown. *Notes on the Earlier History of Barton-on-Humber*, II, 101
1298	Burgesses mentioned—PRO E372/152B m 1

Boston   S

1279	Burgages mentioned—PRO C 133/26/6
1285	Grant of a toll to the bailiffs and burgesses of B—P. Thompson. *History and Antiquities of Boston*, 1854, 43
1545	Charter of Henry VIII incorporating the borough—Weinbaum, 69

Caistor   R

1197–8	Rent of 20 marks from the borough in Pipe Roll. Sums *de incremento fori* had been paid since 1176–7—*Pipe Roll Soc*, NS, IX, 1932, 64, and ibid, XXVI, 1905, 106

Gainsborough   S

1200 × 1250	Charter of John Talbot for the burgesses of G—Ballard & Tait, 56, 74, 217

Grantham   R

1066	111 burgesses, 4 mills, and a church—DB, I, 337*d*
1463	Incorporated—Weinbaum, 70

Grimsby R

1194	Burgesses mentioned—HMC *8th Report*, 1881, 269
1201, 1207	Charters of King John, that of 1207 referring to the king's court of burgesses—Ballard, 10, 82, 87, 117, 133, 135, 136, 142, 144, 147, 150, 153, 181, 196; 125
1202	Represented as a borough by its own jury at the eyre—PRO JI 1/479 mm 1, 9

Lincoln R

c 92	The Roman colonia of *Lindum*
627 × 631	Blaecca, reeve (*praefectus*) of the city, converted to Christianity—Bede. *Hist Eccl*, II, 16
942	A Danish borough annexed by King Edmund—*Anglo-Saxon Chronicle*
1072	An episcopal see
1086	A Domesday city
1154 onwards	A long series of royal charters—*Cal Charter Rolls*, III, 7, 8, 312

Louth E

1086	The bishop of Lincoln has a market, thirteen mills, eighty burgesses—DB, I, 345a

New Sleaford E

1258	116 burgesses—Queen's Coll, Oxon, MS 366, analysed by W. H. Hosford. *Nottingham Medieval Studies*, XII, 1968, 21–39

Stamford R

918	A Danish borough, annexed by Edward the Elder—*Anglo-Saxon Chronicle*
1066, 1086	A Domesday borough—DB, I, 336d

1202	Represented as a borough or vill by its own jury at the eyre—PRO JI 1/479 m 1
1462	Incorporated—Weinbaum, 73

Torksey R

873	Headquarters of a Danish army—*Anglo-Saxon Chronicle*
1066	215 burgesses, reduced by 1086 to 102—DB, 1, 337a

Wainfleet

1458	Incorporated—Weinbaum, 74; also PRO DL41/11/11

Willingthorpe (Lincoln) (alias Westgate) E

1126	Described as a borough—*Registrum Antiquissimum*, Lincs Rec Soc, 1, 188
c 1160	Four dwellings free of all service 'praeter burgagium' —F. M. Stenton. *Documents Illustrative of the Social and Economic History of the Danelaw*, 1920, 343

LONDON

London

	The Roman *Londinium*
673 × 685	The Anglo-Saxon *Lundenwic*, where the king of Kent had a residence and a *wic*-reeve—Laws of Hlothhere and Eadric, cap 16, in F. L. Attenborough. *The Laws of the Earliest English Kings*, 22
1066 × 1075	William I confirms to the burgesses of L the laws of King Edward's day (sc 1043 × 1066), and grants intestate succession to heirs—Ballard, 4 and 74

MIDDLESEX

Uxbridge S

c 1170   Charter of Gilbert Basset granting to his burgesses of
              U toll of all sales made within their houses—G. Redford
              & T. H. Riches. *History of Uxbridge*, 1818, 39

NORFOLK

Castle Rising S

1233 × 1243   Charter of Hugh de Albini—F. Blomefield. *Norfolk*,
              IV, 1775 ed, 620
1243   Payment from the manor and borough—PRO E372/
              92 m 16
1275   Borough rents—PRO C133/10/6

Great Yarmouth R

1066, 1086   Seventy burgesses—DB, II, 118
1208   Charter of King John creating Y a free borough—
              Ballard, 3, 82, 87, 114, 117, 123, 133, 135, 136, 142,
              144, 147, 150, 188, 196, 197, 207, 230, 244

King's Lynn E-R

1204   Charter of John, Bishop of Norwich, creating L a
              free borough with the customs of Oxford—Ballard,
              32
1204   Charter of King John confirming the bishop's grant
              and adding a merchants' guild—Ballard, 3, 13, 31, 32,

35, 82, 87, 114, 117, 123, 133, 135, 136, 142, 144, 147, 150, 188, 196, 197, 207

1524   Incorporated—Weinbaum, 82

New Buckenham   S

c 1170   Founded by William de Albini
1247–8   Described as a borough—PRO E372/92 m 15

Norwich   R

1004   The borough burnt by Swein—*Anglo-Saxon Chronicle*
1066   1,320 burgesses—DB, II, 116
1086   655 English and 160 French burgesses—ibid
1094 × 1096   An episcopal see
1250   A city with its own coroner—PRO JI 1/565 m 35*d*

Thetford   R

952   A great slaughter in the borough of T—*Anglo-Saxon Chronicle*
1004   The borough burnt by Swein—ibid
1066   943 burgesses—DB, II, 118*b*, 119
1072–95   An episcopal see
1086   720 burgesses, 224 empty messuages—DB, II, 118*b*, 119, 136, 137, 173
1250   Represented as a borough, vill, and half-hundred by its own jury at the eyre—PRO JI 1/565 m 23d

NORTHAMPTONSHIRE

Brackley   S

1235 × 1264   Grant by Roger de Quincy of certain liberties to the
burgesses of B—Baker, *Northants*, I, 567

Catesby   S

1493   A reference to burgage here—PRO E326/721

Finedon

1247   Represented as a borough or vill by its own jury at the
eyre—PRO JI 1/614b m 37

Higham Ferrers   S

1251   Created a free borough by William de Ferrers, Earl of
Derby—Ballard & Tait, 47, 142

Northampton   R

1011   Capital of a shire—*Anglo-Saxon Chronicle*
1066   Sixty burgesses—DB, I, 219a
1086   Forty-seven burgesses remaining, and forty in the 'new
borough'—ibid
1189   Charter of Richard I, renewed 1200 by John, granting
the customs of London, with portmoot, fee-farm, and
other privileges—Ballard, 10, 82, 85, 87, 116, 133, 135,
142, 144, 147, 150, 152, 181, 196, 222, 244, 246

Oundle   E

1125 × 1128   Ten burgesses who pay 30s—*Chronicon Petroburgense*,
Camden Soc, XLVII, 1849, 158

Peterborough   E

1125 × 1128 Eighteen burgesses and fifty-five 'homines'—*Chronicon*
Petroburgense, Camden Soc, XLVII, 1849, 161

Rockingham   R

1307 Taxed as a borough—Willard, 433

Rothwell   E

1173 × 1176 A reference to free burgage—*Cartulary of Cirencester*,
ed C. D. Ross, II, 1964, 564, 569
1307 Taxed as a borough—Willard, 433

Towcester   R

  The Roman *Lactodorum*
917 A *burh* fortified by Edward the Elder—*Anglo-Saxon*
Chronicle

NORTHUMBERLAND

Alnmouth   S

1147 Grant by Eustace de Vesci to Alnwick Abbey of a
messuage 'in the borough of St Waleric'—Dugdale,
Monasticon, VI, 867
c 1240 Charter of John de Vesci granting to the Carmelites of
Hulme the right of making purchases in his borough
of A without hindrance from the burgesses—ibid, VI,
1,575

Alnwick   S

1157 × 1185   Charter of William de Vesci granting to his burgesses of A the customs of Newcastle—Ballard, 25

Bamburgh   R

1169–70   Fine paid by a burgess—*Pipe Roll Soc*, xv, 1892, 52
1296   Taxed as a borough—Willard, 433
1332   Grant to the burgesses of a market, two fairs, and a guild merchant—Weinbaum, 88

Berwick   R

1119 × 1124   A Scottish burgh—G. S. Pryde. *The Burghs of Scotland*, 1965, 1
1302   An English borough—*Cal Charter Rolls*, iii, 27–9

Corbridge   R

The Roman *Corstopitum*
1201   Charter of King John granting the fee-farm of the vill to his burgesses of C—Ballard, 227
1296   Taxed as a borough—PRO E179/185/1 m 20

Felton   S

1323   Burgage tenants who in time of peace paid 46s, but now 8s—PRO C134/83/5

Harbottle   S

1245   Borough valued at £2 12s a year—PRO C132/3/9
1308   A borough 'called Hirbotell'—*Cal Inq Post Mortem*, v, 14

Haydon Bridge   S

1365	Burgages on both sides of the water—PRO C135/201/5 and 210/12
1420	Two burgages and one waste burgage—*Cal Inq Misc*, VII, 349
1607	Twenty burgage tenements—PRO LR 2/223

Hexham   E

1547	'Borough' rubric, and burgesses mentioned in a survey—*Northumberland County History*, III, 79

Holy Island   E

1396	Burgages mentioned in an inquisition *post mortem*—PRO Durham 3/2/11 f 123*d*
1466	A burgess of HI receives a grant from the steward of the borough—Raine, *North Durham*, 156 n2

Mitford   S

ND	Quitclaim by the burgesses of M—*Newminster Cartulary*, Surtees Soc, LXVI, 1878, 29
1326	Twenty burgages in M 'as of the castle'—*Cal Inq Post Mortem*, VI, 463

Morpeth   S

1188 × 1239	Charter of Roger de Merlai granting free customs to his burgesses of M—Ballard, 21
1239 × 1266	Charter of Roger de Merlai III extending the area of the borough—Ballard & Tait, 48

Newbiggin on Sea

1307	Taxed as a borough—Willard, 433
1372	A borough—PRO C135/231/3

Newbrough S

c 1320 A new borough in the manor of Thornton—J.
Hodgson. *History of Northumberland*, IV, 1820-58, 383

1369 Burgages recorded—PRO C135/207/12

Newburn

1201 King John granted the town in fee-farm to its burgesses
—*Rot Chart*, 87

1204 Payment of £40 in farm—*Pipe Roll Soc*, NS, XVIII,
1940, 41 (sub 'Nieweburc', indexed as Newburgh: but
sub 'Nieweton', indexed as Newburn, 1206: ibid, XX,
1942)

Newcastle-on-Tyne R

1100 × 1135 Burgesses and burgage—Ballard, 64, 71: original now
PRO C47 34/1/15

1296 Taxed as a borough—Willard, 433

1400 Incorporated as a county borough—Weinbaum, 89

Newton in Warkworth S

1249 A *nova villa*—PRO C132/9/1

1310 Tenements called 'the vill of the new borough'—PRO
C134/17/6

Norham E

1160 × 1180 Bishop Hugh grants the burgesses of N the privileges
of Newcastle on Tyne—Raine, *North Durham*, 257
note h, and Durham, Dean and Chapter Muniments,
Reg I ii f 2v

1183 A borough of the bishop of Durham—DB, IV, 573*b*
(Boldon Book)

Rothbury R

1201 Burgesses farm the borough for £20 pa—*Northumberland County History*, xv, 344

Warenmouth R

1247 Charter of Henry III granting the customs of Newcastle on Tyne to his burgesses of the new borough of W—Ballard & Tait, 21

Warkworth S

1249 Borough farmed for £3 18 7½d—PRO C132/9/1

NOTTINGHAMSHIRE

Newark E

1086 The bishop of Lincoln has in demesne fifty-six burgesses—DB, 1, 283*d*

Nottingham R

918 The borough captured and repaired by Edward the Elder—*Anglo-Saxon Chronicle*
1016 Capital of a shire—ibid
1066 173 burgesses—DB, 1, 280*a*
1086 Thirteen houses built in the new borough—ibid
1157 Charter of Henry II confirming to the burgesses of N all the free customs they had under Henry I—Ballard, 7
1449 Incorporated as a county borough—Weinbaum, 91

Retford R

1259 Charter of Henry III granting an eight-day fair for the improvement of his borough of R. All inhabitants to pay scot and lot with the other burgesses—Ballard & Tait, 139, 250

OXFORDSHIRE

Banbury E

1163 × 1166 House and plot granted in free burgage—*Oseney Cartulary*, Oxf Hist Soc, CI, 1936, vi, 147

1166 Borough mentioned—*Pipe Roll Soc*, XI, 1889, 58

1247 Represented as a borough and vill by its own jury at the eyre—PRO JI 1/700 m 6d

1296 Taxed as a borough—Willard, 433

Burford S

1087 × 1107 Charter of Robert Fitz Hamo granting a merchant guild and other privileges—Ballard, 64, 197, 203

1156 Charter of confirmation by Henry II for the free burgesses of B—ibid, 17

1241 Represented as a borough and vill by its own jury at the eyre—PRO JI 1/695 m 24d

Chinnor S

1338 Conveyance of a burgage located next to two others—*VCH Oxon*, VIII, 66

1578–9 Burgages mentioned—ibid

Chipping Norton

1296 Taxed as a borough—Willard, 433

Eynsham
E

1215   Charter of Adam, Abbot of E, granting to the burgesses of E the liberties and customs of the burgesses of Oxford—Ballard, 34, 74

1366   Thirty-one houses in the new borough and some 300 in the old town—*Eynsham Cartulary*, Oxf Hist Soc, XLIX, 1906, xliv, and LI, 1908, 50–6, 177

Henley-on-Thames
R

1179   The king buys land at H for building purposes—*Pipe Roll Soc*, XXVIII, 1907, 95

1241   Represented as a borough and vill by its own jury at the eyre—PRO JI 1/695 m 1

1296   Taxed as a borough—Willard, 433

1300   Burgage rents—PRO C133/95

Oxford
R

c 900   A *burh* with 1,500 hides ascribed to it in the *Burghal Hidage*—Robertson, *Anglo-Saxon Charters*, 246

1011   Capital of a shire—*Anglo-Saxon Chronicle*

1066   A city with burgesses and 721 houses—DB, 1, 154*a*

1156   Charter of Henry II confirming the liberties and customs his citizens of O had under Henry I—Ballard, 6, 13

Thame
E

1230 × 1234   Sixty-three burgages recorded *VCH Oxon*, VII, 13

1247   Represented as a borough and vill by its own jury at the eyre—PRO JI 1/700 m 3*d*

1258   Seventy-six burgages listed—Queen's Coll, Oxon, MS 366, ff 23*d*–25

Witney

E

1208–9	20s paid from the borough *pro pace habenda*—Hants RO Eccles 2/159270, under *purchasia*
1210–11	Reeve of the borough—ibid, Eccles 2/159270B, m 4
1213–14	First separate account for borough—ibid, Eccles 2/159272
1241	Represented as a borough and vill by its own jury at the eyre—PRO JI 1/695 m 25
1296	Taxed as a borough—Willard, 433

Woodstock

R

1230	Rents paid from the borough—*Pipe Roll Soc*, NS, IV, 1927, 258
1241	Represented as a borough and vill by its own jury at the eyre—PRO JI 1/695 m 25
1453	Incorporated

RUTLAND

Oakham

R

1297	Farm of six burgages in O—L. M. Midgley, ed. *Ministers' Accounts of the Earldom of Cornwall, 1296–7*, Camden Soc, 3rd ser, LXVII, 1945, 159
1300	Twenty-nine burgesses—*Cal Inq Post Mortem*, III, 461
1373	Portmoot mentioned—*VCH Rutland*, 7

SHROPSHIRE

Acton Burnell   S

c 1269–70   Charter of Robert Burnell founding a borough at AB
—Salop RO, 1514/6

Albrighton   S

1303   Ralph de Pichford had jurisdiction over his burgesses
in A—Eyton, *Shropshire*, II, 156

1663   Charter of incorporation by Charles II referring to A
as an ancient borough with a court distinct from that
of A. Foreign. Copy in parish records

Baschurch   E

1227   Charter of Henry III referring to the church of 'Novus
Burgus'—Dugdale, *Monasticon*, III, 522

1339   Grant of burgages in 'Nova Villa de Baschurch'—
Eyton, *Shropshire*, X, 133

Bishop's Castle   E

1285   Forty-six burgages recorded—*Red Book of Hereford*,
Camden Soc, 3rd ser, XLI, 1929, 29, 30

Bridgnorth   R

1100 × 1135   Charter of Henry II (1157) granting to his burgesses of
B all the liberties and customs they had under Henry I
—Ballard, 12
See also Quatford, p 153

Burford   S

1265–6   Charters of Hugh de Mortimer and Henry III creating
                B a free borough—Eyton, *Shropshire*, IV, 318

Caus   S

1273   Twenty-eight burgages recorded—PRO C133/7/8

Cleobury Mortimer   S

1362   Grant of a burgage in the new street of C—*Trans
                Shrop Arch Soc*, II, 1879, 62
1509   Draft court roll of the borough—Birmingham Ref
                Lib, Childe MS 56/1

Clun   S

1272   183 + 22 burgages recorded—PRO C132/42/5

Ellesmere   S

1216 × 1237   Charter of Joan of Wales granting to the borough of
                E the customs of Breteuil—Ballard, 20
1338   Charter of Robert Strange, Lord of E, creating a new
                borough at E and including the old borough in it—
                eighteenth-century translation of lost original, Salop
                RO

Ludlow   R

1300   Grant of a burgage in L within the liberty of the town
                —Merewether and Stephens. *History of the Boroughs
                and Municipal Corporations of the UK*, I, 1835, 527
1461   Incorporated as a free borough—Weinbaum, 96

Lydham S

1270   Charter of Henry III granting to Adam de Mont-
        gomery a free borough at L—Ballard & Tait, 3, 132,
        176, 247, 249, 260

Madeley E

1426   Deed referring to a burgage with a messuage on it—
        Salop RO, 1142/1

Market Drayton E

ND (late   Grants of burgages by the abbot of Combermere—
thirteenth   Eyton, *Shropshire*, IX, 187–8
cent)
1292   The abbot of Combermere has in the town of Drayton
        in tithes of the new borough £10—*Taxatio Ecclesiastica*,
        261

Newport R

1159   'Aid' from borough recorded on the Pipe Roll—Eyton,
        Shropshire, IX, 129
1100 × 1135   Charter of Henry II (1163 × 1166) confirming to his
        burgesses of 'Novus Burgus' all the liberties and cus-
        toms they had under Henry I—Ballard, 17

Oswestry S

1190 × 1200   Charter of William fitz William fitz Alan granting
        protection to his burgesses of 'Blancmoster' (ie O),
        especially those who have taken messuages from his
        bailiff for the improvement of his market—Ballard, 81

Quatford   R

912	A borough built at Bridgnorth by Aethelflaed of Mercia—*Anglo-Saxon Chronicle*
1086	'A new house and the borough called Q pays nothing' —DB, I, 254*a*
1101	The borough removed to Bridgnorth, the bounds of which included Q

Richard's Castle   S

See under Herefordshire (p 123)

Ruyton   S

1308	Charter of Edmund, Earl of Arundel, founding a borough at R—Weinbaum, 98
1304 × 1310	Record of seven burgages in the 'nova villa' at R— Eyton, *Shropshire*, x, 111

Shifnal   ?S

1441	Grant of half a burgage in S—BM Eg MS 3712, f 41

Shrewsbury   R

901	Described as a city—Birch, *Cart Sax*, no 587
1006	Capital of a shire—*Anglo-Saxon Chronicle*
1066	252 houses and 252 burgesses—DB, I, 252*a*

Stottesdon

1619	Conveyance of a burgage—Salop RO, 1037
1684	Conveyance of 3½ burgages—ibid

Wenlock   E

1203	Represented as a borough and vill by its own jury at the eyre—PRO JI 1/732 m 2*d*
1247	Thirty-nine burgesses—Eyton, *Shropshire*, III, 257
1468	Incorporated—Weinbaum, 100

SOMERSET

Axbridge   R

c 900	A *burh* with 400 hides assigned to it in the *Burghal Hidage*—Robertson, *Anglo-Saxon Charters*, 246
1086	Thirty-six burgesses—DB, 1, 86*b*
1243	Represented as a borough by its own jury at the eyre —PRO JI 1/756 m 14*d*

Badgworth

| 1243 | Represented as a borough by four jurors of its own at the eyre—PRO JI 1/756 m 14*d* |

Bath   R

	The Roman *Aquae Sulis* or *Aquae Calidae*
c 675	A city with 100 hides appurtenant to it—Birch, *Cart Sax*, no 43
c 900	A *burh* with 1,000 hides assigned to it in the *Burghal Hidage*—Robertson, *Anglo-Saxon Charters*, 246
1066	A borough of 20 hides—DB, 1, 87*b*
1500	Incorporated—Weinbaum, 101

Bridgwater   S

1200 Charter of King John granting to William Brewer a free borough at B, with free burgesses, a market and other privileges—Ballard, 3, 101, 171, 174, 176, 189

Bruton   R

1086 Five burgesses belonging to the king and eleven to Thurstin fitz Rolf—DB, I, 86c, 97c

Chard   E

1234 Charter to Joscelyn, Bishop of Wells, creating a free borough at C; confirmed 1286 by Edward I—*Cal Pat Rolls, 1281–92*, 216

1306 onwards Taxed as a borough—Willard, 433

Down End   S

1159 Philip de Columbers owes 10s for *burgriht*—*Pipe Roll Soc*, I, 1884, 20, possibly referring to this place

1225 Represented as the borough of *Chef del Munt* or *Caput Montis* by its own jury at the eyre—PRO JI 1/755 m 3d

Dunster   S

1197 £21 from the borough of D—*Pipe Roll Soc*, XLVI, 1931, 138–9

1225 Represented as a borough by its own jury at the eyre— PRO JI 1/755 m 3

1254 × 1257 Charter of Reginald de Mohun granting privileges to the burgesses of D—Ballard & Tait, 6, 76, 107, 109, 117, 130, 218, 265, 299, 330

Glastonbury   E

1319	Parliamentary borough
1517	A portmoot held twice yearly—*Johannes Glastoniensis Chronica*, II, ed T. Hearne, Oxford, 1726, 308

Ilchester   R

The Roman *Lindinis*

1086	107 burgesses, paying the king 20s—DB, I, 86c
1204	Charter of King John, confirming a lost charter of Henry II, which granted to the burgesses of I all the customs of Winchester—Ballard, 11, 14, 114, 120, 137, 169, 174, 190, 229

Langport   R

c 900	A *burh* with 600 hides assigned to it in the *Burghal Hidage*—Robertson, *Anglo-Saxon Charters*, 246
1086	Thirty-four burgesses paying the king 15s—DB, I, 86b
1225	Represented as a borough by its own jury at the eyre— PRO JI 1/755 m 4

Lyng   R

c 900	A *burh* with 100 hides assigned to it in the *Burghal Hidage*—Robertson, *Anglo-Saxon Charters*, 246

Merryfield   S

1275	A rental of East Coker includes 16s 8d from the borough of *Murifeud* (?Merryfield in Ilton)—*Cal Inq Post Mortem*, II, 97

Milborne Port   R

1086   Fifty-six burgesses and a market paying 60s—DB, I,
          86c
1225   Represented as a borough and manor by its own jury
          at the eyre—PRO JI 1/755 m 3

Milverton   S

1280   Represented as a borough, manor, and vill by its own
          jury at the eyre—PRO JI 1/761 m 3
1306 onwards Taxed as a borough—Willard, 434

Montacute   E

1102   Charter of William, Count of Mortain, founding a
          priory at M and endowing it with, *inter alia*, the
          borough and its market tolls—*Somerset Rec Soc*, VIII,
          1894, 119

Nether Stowey   S

1225   Represented as a borough and vill by its own jury at
          the eyre—PRO JI 1/755 m 3d
1275–6   A free borough—*Rotuli Hundredorum*, II, 127
1306 onwards Taxed as a borough—Willard, 434

Newport (in North Curry)   E

1349   Grant of a burgage and half-burgage in N—HMC.
          Dean and Chapter of Wells, I, 1907, 417

Rackley (in Compton Bishop)   E

1179   Confirmation by Pope Alexander III to the bishop of
          Bath of the vill of Compton with the port of 'Rade-
          clife'—HMC. *Dean and Chapter of Wells*, I, 1907,
          438–40

1189	Charter of Richard I allowing the bishop to make a borough on his land of 'Radeclive'—Ballard & Tait, 378, 380

Redcliff S

1247	Charter to Henry III giving the burgesses of R the right to answer with Bristol before the king's justices—*Cal Charter Rolls, 1226–57*, 325

Somerton R

1313, 1315, 1319	Taxed at the urban rate as a borough; as a vill but at the borough rate, 1332–6—Willard, 434
1330	Divers burgesses in the 'new borough' pay £6 14s 0d rent—PRO C135/24

Stoford S

1273	74½ burgages in the borough of S—PRO C133/2/7
1332, 1334, 1336	Taxed as a borough—Willard, 434

Stogursey S

1225	Represented as a borough by its own jury at the eyre—PRO JI 1/755 m 2
1306 onwards	Taxed as a borough—Willard, 434

Taunton E

934 × 951	Bishop of Winchester granted market tolls and burgage rents—H. P. R. Finberg. *The Early Charters of Wessex*, 1964, 217–44
964 × 970	Bishop granted full seignorial jurisdiction, including the profits of justice—ibid
1086	Sixty-four burgesses paying the bishop 32s; a market paying 50s—DB, I, 86c

1135 × 1139   Charter of Stephen granting to the bishop's burgesses of T the customs of London and Winchester—Ballard, 12

Templemead   E

1306 onwards   Taxed as a borough—Willard, 434

Watchet   R

c 900   A *burh* with 513 hides assigned to it in the *Burghal Hidage*—Robertson, *Anglo-Saxon Charters*, 246

988   A port, sacked by the Danes—*Anglo-Saxon Chronicle*

1225   Represented as a borough by its own jury at the eyre— PRO JI 1/175 m 1*d*

1306 onwards   Taxed as a borough—Willard, 434

Weare (Nether)   S

1243   Represented as a borough and manor by six jurors of its own at the eyre—PRO JI 1/756 m 16

1265   Described as a borough—*Cal Inq Misc*, 1, 266

1278–9   Charter of Edward I granting to the burgesses of NW the customs of Hereford and Breteuil—Ballard & Tait, 24, 105, 160, 261

Wellington   E

1330   Named as a borough by the keepers of the estates of the bishopric of Bath and Wells—PRO E326/B 9624/2

1345   Grant to the burgesses of W—*Cal Pat Rolls, 1343–5*, 466

Wells   E

909 onwards   An episcopal see

1174 × 1180   Charter of Bishop Reginald, confirming one by Bishop Robert (1136–66) creating a borough at W— Ballard, 2, 65, 112, 212

Wiveliscombe E

1301   Described as a borough—PRO SC 6/1131 m 3

Yeovil E

1305–6   Charter of Robert de la More, rector and lord of the town, granting to his burgesses a portmote and the right of electing their own reeve—Ballard & Tait, 181, 357

STAFFORDSHIRE

Abbot's Bromley E

1222   Charter of Richard, Abbot of Burton, stating that Henry III has given him leave to make a borough in the vill of B; he accordingly grants burgage tenure at 12d a year and all the customs of Lichfield—Ballard & Tait, 18, 45, 63, 70, 123

Alton

1239   Pasturage agreement between burgesses of A and Croxden Abbey—Staffs RO, D593/A/2/23/1, with borough seal

1316   Burgesses paying 40s rent in inquisition post mortem—*Staffs Hist Coll, 1911,* 334

Betley

1299   Many burgages listed in inquisition post mortem—*Staffs Hist Coll, 1908,* 248–9

Brewood   E

c 1280   Grant of a burgage—Salt Library S MS 201 (1), quoted *VCH Staffs*, v, 36

Burton-on-Trent   E

1187 × 1197   Abbot Nicholas made 'the first borough of Burton, that is the vill and the new street'. Successive abbots (1260–81 and 1281–1305) 'made boroughs' by extending burghality to streets—Dugdale, *Monasticon*, III, 48

1200 × 1214   Charter of William, Abbot of Burton, stating that the king has given him leave to make a borough at B from the Great Bridge to the New Bridge, with all the liberties belonging to a borough—Ballard, 21, 42, 49, 51

Church Eaton

1275   Free borough in inquisition post mortem—*Staffs Hist Coll, 1911*, 163

Colton   S

1275   Release of right in a burgage in the vill of C—(F. P. Parker). *Some Account of Colton and of the de Wasteneys Family* (privately pr, Birmingham, 1897), 314

1361   16s 7d received by the de Wasteneys' steward for half a year's rent from the burgesses—ibid, 79

Eccleshall   E

1199   Represented as a manor and borough by its own jury at the eyre—PRO JI 1/800 m 3

1240–1   A burgage next to the fishyard and to another burgage—*Staffs Hist Coll, 1924*, 255

1298	Survey gives 57¾ burgages—Staffs RO, D1734 J2268
1313	Taxed as a borough—Willard, 434

Kinver S

ND (thirteenth cent)	Charter of John fitz John fitz Philip allowing all his burgesses of K to hold their burgages as freely as the burgesses of Kidderminster hold theirs, for 10d yearly— S. Shaw. *Staffordshire*, II, 1801, 262

Leek S–E

c 1214	Charter of Ranulf de Blundeville, Earl of Chester, granting to his free burgesses of L the liberties of the freest burgesses in Staffordshire—Ballard, 22, 33, 44, 50, 57, 62, 68, 157, 178, 194, 246
After 1224	Charter of Richard, Abbot of Dieulacres, confirming the foregoing—Ballard & Tait, 31, 56, 85, 263

Lichfield E

669	Seat of a bishopric
1155–9	Two dwellings in the borough—*Staffs Hist Coll, 1924, 1926,* 87
1176	A burgage on the causeway—ibid, 78
1199	Represented as a borough, vill, and liberty by its own jury at the eyre—PRO JI 1/800 m 3
1307 onwards	Taxed as a borough—Willard, 434

Newborough (Agardsley) S

1263	Charter of Robert de Ferrers III, Earl of Derby, granting two acres of arable land and one acre for building in his free borough of A, with the customs of Stafford— Ballard & Tait, 23, 47, 57, 77, 113, 118, 124, 129, 179, 266
1301	101 burgages—PRO DL29/1/3 m 5

New Borough (? in Tutbury)   S

?1100 × 1139   Charter of Robert de Ferrers II, Earl of Derby (1141), granting to Tutbury Priory tithe of the burgage rents in the new borough which his father had caused to grow—*William Salt Arch Soc*, 4th ser, IV, 1962, 75

1150 × 1159   Charter of the same expressing his intention of making the new borough grow further—ibid, 65

c 1150   Grant of a burgage in N—ibid, 78

On the assumption that this *novus burgus* of the de Ferrers is distinct from that of the 1263 charter, above —*VCH Staffs*, II, 349. It may be the Newbiggin of PRO SC 12/14/80, DL42/4 and DL42/109

Newcastle-under-Lyne (see also ADDENDA, p 193)   R

1173   The borough contributes tallage—*Staffs Hist Coll*, I, 1880, 69

1203   Represented as a borough by its own jury at the eyre—PRO JI 1/799 m 3

1235   Charter of Henry III making N a free borough—Ballard & Tait, 3, 257, 280, 289

Penkridge

c 1290   Burgages conveyed in deeds—*Staffs Hist Coll*, *1931*, *1933*, 242, 245–6

Stafford   R

913   A *burh* built by Aethelflaed of Mercia—*Anglo-Saxon Chronicle*

1016   A shire town—ibid

1086   Eighteen burgesses, 161 houses (51 of which were waste), eighteen extramural burgesses—DB, I, 246a, 247c, 248 (bis), 248c (bis)

| 1199 | Represented as a borough and vill by its own jury at the eyre—PRO JI 1/800 m 3 |
| 1206 | Charter of King John granting a free borough at S—Ballard, 3, 15, 109, 115, 120, 123, 137, 144, 164, 188 |

Stone   E

| 1364 | Transfer of half a burgage—*Wm Salt Lib*, MS 264/38 |
| 1536 | Burgages mentioned—Abstract of Stone Cartulary, *Staffs Hist Coll*, VI, pt 1, 1885, 3 |

Tamworth   R

913	A *burh* built by Aethelflaed of Mercia—*Anglo-Saxon Chronicle*
1086	Incidental references to burgesses—DB, I, 238*b*, 246*b*, 246*d*
1199	Represented as a borough and vill by its own jury at the eyre—PRO JI 1/800 m 3
1307 onwards	Taxed as a borough—Willard, 107

Tutbury   S

1086	'In the borough round the castle' forty-two men 'living by their market alone'—DB, I, 248*c*
1141	Mentioned as 'the old borough' in relation to New Borough (p 162)—*Staffs Arch Coll*, 4th ser, IV, 1962, 75
1199	Represented as a borough, manor, and vill by its own jury at the eyre—PRO JI 1/800 m 3

Uttoxeter   S

| 1252 | Charter of William, Earl of Derby, creating a free borough and free burgages at U—Ballard & Tait, 3, 56, 74, 117, 135, 141, 264, 287, 325 |

Walsall S

c 1198   Charter of William Ruffus granting to the burgesses of
         W burgage tenure at a rent of 12d, with other privi-
         leges—Ballard, 43, 49, 60, 69, 158, 239

Wolverhampton E

1263   The dean of W grants his burgesses of W privileges
         similar to those of Stafford—Staffs RO, D593B 1/26/
         6/34/1

SUFFOLK

Beccles R

1086   Twenty-six burgesses and a market—DB, II, 369*b*,
         370, 283*b*
1238   Represented as a borough and vill by its own jury at
         the eyre—PRO JI 1/819 m 39

Bungay

1228   Represented as a borough and vill by its own jury at
         the eyre—PRO JI 1/819 m 39

Bury St Edmunds E

1022 × 1043   *Seynt Eadmundes biri—Anglo-Saxon Wills*, ed D. White-
              lock, 1930, 74
1102–3   Charter of Henry I confirming the monastery and
              burgesses in all the liberties they enjoyed under Cnut
              and Edward the Confessor—Ballard, 15, 121, 180

1135 × 1154   Charter of Stephen exempting the men of the borough from all taxation except when levied by the abbey—Ballard, 91

Clare   S

1086   Forty-three burgesses—DB, II, 389*b*

1262   Survey of borough—*Cal Inq Post Mortem*, I, 154

Dunwich   R

803   A city—Birch, *Cart Sax*, no 312

1066   A borough with 120 burgesses—DB, II, 311*b*, 312, 331*b*, 333*b*, 385*b*

1200   Charter of King John creating D a free borough, with merchant guild and other privileges—Ballard, 3, 67, 77, 114, 123, 124, 188, 206, 225

Exning

1228   Represented as a half-hundred, borough, and vill by its own jury at the eyre—PRO JI 1/819 m 39

Eye

1086   Twenty-five burgesses—DB, II, 319*b*, 320, 379, 449*b*

1228   Represented as a borough and vill by its own jury at the eyre—PRO JI 1/819 m 39

1408   Annexed (? in error) the charter of Hythe, Kent—*Cal Pat Rolls, 1405-8*, 392: *ex inf* Mr D. Charman

Ipswich   R

1066   538 burgesses—DB, II, 290

1200   Charter of King John granting a merchant guild, the right to elect a coroner and to hold the town in fee-farm, and other privileges—Ballard, 14, 82, 87, 117, 135, 144, 153, 188, 195, 206, 226, 245, 247

| 1228 | Represented as a borough by its own jury at the eyre—PRO JI 1/819 m 39 |

Orford   R

1256	Charter of liberties granted by Henry III—HMC. *Var Coll*, IV, 1907, 256–7
1306	Burgages pay 6d rent for half-year—PRO SC 6/1003/3
1294, 1306, 1315	Taxed at the urban rate as a vill; as a borough 1313, 1316 onwards—Willard, 434
	In 1193–4 the men of Orford paid for having a charter, contents unspecified—*Pipe Roll Soc*, NS, V, 1928, 64

Southwold

| 1490 | Incorporated—Weinbaum, 111 |

Sudbury

| 1086 | Sixty-three burgesses dwelling by the hall and fifty-five on the demesne—DB, II, 286b |

SURREY

Blechingley   S

1226	A malefactor dwelling in the borough of B—PRO JI 1/863 m 5
1235	Represented as a borough and vill by its own jury at the eyre—PRO JI 1/864 m 3
1294 onwards	Taxed as a borough

Eashing

| c 900 | A *burh* to which 600 hides are assigned in the *Burghal Hidage*—Robertson, *Anglo-Saxon Charters*, 246 |

Farnham   E

1208–9	Farm of the borough, £7—Hants RO Eccles 2/159270A
1225	Named separately from the manor in the accounts of the bishop of Winchester—ibid, 2/159280
1241	A borough in the roll of the eyre—PRO JI 1/867 m 17
1247	Charter of William, Bishop of Winchester, confirming the existing privileges of the borough—Ballard & Tait, 16, 146, 173, 178, 221, 250, 252, 312, 352

Gatton

| 1450 | A Parliamentary borough—*VCH Surrey*, III, 197 |

Guildford   R

1130–1	Borough of G pays an aid of £5—Joseph Hunter, ed. *Magnus rotulus scaccarii*, 1833, 52
1129 × 1135	Writ of Henry I addressed to the reeves and burgesses of G—Ballard, 106
1235	Represented as a borough or vill by its own jury at the eyre—PRO JI 1/864 m 14*d*

Haslemere   R

| 1230 | Grant of a burgage—E. W. Swanton & P. Woods. *Bygone Haslemere*, 1914, 49 |
| 1377 | Called a borough—PRO SC 6/1010/7 |

Kingston   R

| 1241 | The name of the bailiff of the borough entered and deleted in the calendar of the eyre—PRO JI 1/867 m 17 |
| 1256 | Charter of Henry III empowering the burgesses to |

keep their guild merchant and to elect their own coroner—Ballard & Tait, 92, 151, 159, 171, 193, 282, 359

Reigate S

1164 × 1202   Charter of Hamelin, Earl of Warenne, granting 10 acres of his demesne to the priory of St Mary Overy in exchange for a burgage belonging to the priory—Dugdale, *Monasticon*, VI, 172

1235   Represented as a borough and vill by its own jury at the eyre—PRO JI 1/864 m 15*d*

Southwark R

c 900   A *burh* to which 1,800 hides are assigned in the *Burghal Hidage*—Robertson, *Anglo-Saxon Charters*, 246

1235   Represented as a borough or vill by its own jury at the eyre—PRO JI 1/864 m 18*d*

1294 onwards Taxed as a borough—Willard, 434

SUSSEX

Arundel S

1086   Four burgesses and thirteen messuages—DB, I, 23*a*

1248   Represented as a borough or vill by its own jury at the eyre—PRO JI 1/909^A m 22*d*

1294 onwards Taxed as a borough—Willard, 434

Battle E

c 1180   The men of the town called burgesses—*Chronicon Monasterii de Bello*, ed J. S. Brewer, 1846, 12–18

Bramber   S

1248	Represented as a borough and vill by a jury of its own at the eyre—PRO JI 1/909^A m 24d
1294 onwards	Taxed as a borough—Willard, 434

Burpham   R

c 900	A *burh* with 720 hides assigned to it in the *Burghal Hidage*—Robertson, *Anglo-Saxon Charters*, 246

Chichester   R

43	The Roman *Noviomagus Regnensium*
1066	A city—DB, I, 23a
1075	An episcopal see
1135 × 1154	Charter of Stephen confirming the rights of his burgesses of C in the borough and merchant guild as they had them in the time of Earl Roger (d 1094)—Ballard, 4

East Grinstead

1235	A reference to the borough of (E)G—*Cal Close Rolls, 1234–37*, 215
1248	Represented as a borough by its own jury at the eyre—PRO JI 1/909^A m 27d
1295 onwards	Taxed as a borough—Willard, 434

Hastings   R

c 900	A *burh* with 500 hides assigned to it in the *Burghal Hidage*—Robertson, *Anglo-Saxon Charters*, 246
1086	Four burgesses—DB, I, 176
1155 × 1158	Charter of Henry II to his barons of H as free men—Ballard, 90

Horsham

1235	Borough of H mentioned—*Cal Close Rolls, 1234-37,* 215
1248	Represented as a borough or vill by its own jury at the eyre—PRO JI 1/909ᴬ m 24
1295 onwards	Taxed as a borough—Willard, 434

Lewes   R

c 900	A *burh* with 1,200 hides assigned to it in the *Burghal Hidage*—Robertson, *Anglo-Saxon Charters,* 246
1066	127 burgesses—DB, 1, 26a
1148	Charter of Reginald de Warenne restoring to the burgesses of L their merchant guild—Ballard, 203

Midhurst

1248	Represented as a borough or vill by its own jury at the eyre—PRO JI 1/909ᴬ m 22d
1279	Said to have been a borough from time immemorial—*Placita de Quo Warranto,* 756

Pevensey   R-S

1066	Twenty-four burgesses on the king's demesne, and twenty-eight other burgesses—DB, 1, 20c
1086	Sixty burgesses on the count of Mortain's demesne, and fifty other burgesses—ibid

Rye   E

1086	In the manor of *Rameslie* is a new borough with sixty-four burgesses—DB, 1, 17b
1189 × 1219	Charter of Ralph, Abbot of Fécamp, confirming the privileges of the burgesses of R—Ballard 97, 111, 160, 234

Seaford

1235	Borough of S mentioned—*Cal Close Rolls, 1234–37*, 215
1248	Represented as a borough or vill by its own jury at the eyre—PRO JI 1/909^A m 29*d*

Shoreham

1208–9	Tallage of the borough—*Pipe Roll Soc*, NS, XXIV, 1948, 4
1235	Borough of S mentioned—*Cal Close Rolls, 1234–37*, 215
1248	Represented as a borough or vill by its own jury at the eyre—PRO JI 1/909^A m 25

Steyning   R

1066	In the borough 118 houses (123 in 1086)—DB, I, 17*b*
1248	Represented as a borough by its own jury at the eyre—PRO JI 1/909^A m 24

Winchelsea   R

1283	Charter of Edward I granting the liberties of Old Winchelsea to those of its barons who settle in the new town—Ballard & Tait, 25. These granted to 'men' of (Old) Winchelsea in 1191—Ballard, 90, 100, 123, 136, 187

WARWICKSHIRE

Alcester   R

1207	Burgage mentioned in deed—Bloom MS, LVII, Birmingham Ref Lib
1251–2	Stated to have been a free borough since the time of Henry II (not Henry I, as in *VCH Warws*, III, 13), who gave it to Robert Corbet
1306 onwards	Taxed as a borough (but styled vill 1319, 1334)—Willard, 435

Atherstone   S

ND (mid-thirteenth cent)	13½ burgages in A—BM Add MS 24316, f 50v
1289	Nine new burgages—King's College, Cambridge, MS C9

Birmingham   S

c 1250	Burgess mentioned—Birmingham Ref Lib, MS 120822
1306, 1307	Taxed as a borough—Willard, 435

Bretford   S

1279	Nineteen burgesses hold 31½ burgages—PRO E164/15, f 11v

Brinklow   S

1306 onwards	Taxed at the urban rate; styled borough 1307, 1315, 1316, 1322, 1332, 1336; vill 1306, 1313, 1319, 1334—Willard, 435

Coleshill S

ND (before 1290) A burgage tenement mentioned—Birmingham Ref Lib, Wingfield-Digby Coll, no 59

Coventry S

1149 × 1153 Charter of Ralph II, Earl of Chester, conferring on the burgesses of C the customs of Lincoln—Ballard, 19, 27, 40, 118, 153, 198, 242

1345 Incorporated—Weinbaum, 116

Henley-in-Arden S

1265 Town burned—*Cal Inq Misc*, I, 931

1296 Sixty-nine burgesses—PRO C133/76/4

Kenilworth S

c 1125 Charter of Henry I confirming to Kenilworth Priory the gifts of its founder, Geoffrey de Clinton, including K itself except the land which he kept in demesne for making his borough—Dugdale, *Monasticon*, VI, 223

Kineton

1306 onwards Taxed at the urban rate, but styled vill; borough in 1313—Willard, 435

1332 Burgages mentioned—*Cal Inq Post Mortem*, VI, 429

Nuneaton E

1227 Charter of Sibyl, Prioress, and Robert, Prior of N, granting that all who hold burgages from them in the town shall hold them as freely as the burgesses of the prior of Coventry hold theirs—PRO E40/A5785

Solihull

c 1280
A burgage held freely according to the customs of Birmingham—Birthplace Lib, Stratford on Avon, Archer Collection, Solihull Charters, D18

1300–1475
Several references to the borough—Records of Solihull United Charities, Warws RO, CR84/26, CR84/23/30, etc

Southam   E

1399–1400
Free burgesses in *Neulonde* hold burgages for rent and various services—PRO E164/21, ff 251v–253r

Stratford on Avon   E

1196
Charter of John, Bishop of Worcester, creating a market at S and granting burgages to all who would come and occupy them—Ballard, 43, 48, 51, 193

Tamworth

See Staffordshire (p 164)

Warwick   R

914
A *burh* built by Aethelflaed of Mercia—*Anglo-Saxon Chronicle*

1001
Charter of Ethelred II granting *inter alia* a messuage (*haga*) in W—Kemble, *Codex Diplomaticus*, no 705

1016
A shire town—*Anglo-Saxon Chronicle*

1086
The king has 113 houses and his barons another 112 in the borough—DB, I, 238*a*, 241*d*, 242*a*, 244*b*

1306 onwards
Taxed as a borough—Willard, 435

WESTMORLAND

Appleby   R

1179   Charter of Henry II granting to his burgesses of A all
            the liberties and free customs of York—Ballard, 27
1200   Charter of King John to the same effect, and granting
            the right to hold the borough in fee-farm—ibid, 27,
            188, 226

Kendal   S

1222 × 1246 Charter of William de Lancaster for his free burgesses
            of Kirkby in Kendal—Ballard & Tait, 14

Market Brough   R

1196   Tallage paid by burgesses; again in 1202—*Pipe Roll
            Soc*, NS, VII, 98; IX, 140; XII, 34; XIV, 257; XV, 156–7

WILTSHIRE

Amesbury   S

1314   Lease by a burgess of A—R. B. Pugh. 'Calendar of
            Antrobus Deeds', *Wilts Arch & Nat Hist Soc Rec Br*,
            III, 1947

Bedwyn   R

1086   Twenty-five burgesses—DB, I, 64*d*
1194   Represented as a borough or vill by its own jury at the
            eyre—PRO KB26/3 m 6

Bradford-on-Avon
E

1086	Thirty-three burgesses—DB, I, 67b
1295	Two burgesses summoned to parliament (for the only time)
1546	Portmote leased with the hundred—*VCH Wilts*, VII, 38
	In 1001 Ethelred II granted the nuns of Shaftesbury a place that would be 'an impenetrable refuge from the barbarians'

Calne
R

1086	Forty-five burgesses—DB, I, 64d
1194	Represented as a borough or inner hundred jointly with the out-hundred at the eyre—PRO KB26/3
1306 onwards	Taxed as a borough—Willard, 435

Chippenham
R

1154 × 1189	The borough was once in the hands of Henry III's grandfather—*Rotuli Hundredorum*, II, 231
1255	Represented as a borough by its own jury—ibid, *loc cit*
1306 onwards	Taxed as a borough (but styled vill in 1315)—Willard, 435

Chisbury

See Tisbury (p 180)

Cricklade
R

| c 900 | A *burh* with 1,400 hides assigned to it in the *Burghal Hidage*—Robertson, *Anglo-Saxon Charters*, 246 |
| 1306 onwards | Taxed as a borough—Willard, 435 |

Devizes E

1135 × 1139   Borough with castle and park established by Roger, Bishop of Salisbury—*Sarum Charters*, Rolls Ser, XLVII, 1891, 22

1135 × 1154   Charter of the Empress Matilda exempting her burgesses of D from payment of toll—Ballard, 80, 181

1157   Henry II acquires the castle, two parks, and the borough by exchange with the bishop of Salisbury—*Sarum Charters*, 29

Downton E

1210–11   Rents of plots in the borough of the bishop of Winchester—Hants RO, Eccles 2/159270 B m 2

Heytesbury S

1168   The men of H paid tallage—*Pipe Roll Soc*, XII, 1890, 161

1449   Parliamentary borough. The borough was West Heytesbury—Sir Richard Hoare. *Modern Wiltshire: The Hundred of Heytesbury*, 1824, 85–7

Highworth S

1262   Fifty tenants held burgages or part-burgages—PRO C132/29/2 m 26

1274   Burgesses mentioned in portmote roll—PRO SC 2/208/81 m 2

1298, 1311   Parliamentary borough

Hindon E

1219–20   A croft and 1½ virgates taken as land for the new borough created by the bishop of Winchester—Hants RO Eccles 2/159276 m 80

Lacock   E

1239 × 1257	Burgage tenements, *temp* Abbess Ela—*Cal Ancient Deeds*, IV, no A9364
1257	Grant of market and fair to Abbess Ela—*Cal Charter Rolls*, I, 274
c 1280	Burgesses and burgages mentioned—*Cal Ancient Deeds*, V, A11183
1283	A burgage conveyed—ibid, IV, no A9244; see also undated deed, no 10899

Ludgershall   S

1194	Represented as a borough by its own jury at the eyre—PRO KB26/3
1306 onwards	Taxed as a borough (styled vill in 1315)—Willard, 435

Malmesbury   R

c 900	A *burh* with 1,200 hides assigned to it in the *Burghal Hidage*—Robertson, *Anglo-Saxon Charters*, 246
1086	A royal borough—DB, I, 64*c*
1249	Represented as a borough by its own jury at the eyre—PRO JI 1/996 m 23

Marlborough   R

1204	Charter of King John, creating a borough at M with the customs of Winchester and Oxford—Ballard, 31, 35, 43, 78, 84, 85, 98, 114, 120, 123, 133, 136, 145, 151, 165, 171, 172, 187, 198, 207

Mere   R

1304	Parliamentary borough

Old Sarum   R

1003   Moneyers at S; a mint in 1086—*VCH Wilts*, VI, 51–3
1075   An episcopal see
1100 × 1135 Charter of Henry I granting a merchant guild—
            Ballard, 185, 205
1194   Represented as a borough by its own jury at the eyre—
            PRO KB26/3

Salisbury   E

1219   Founded by Richard Poore, Bishop of S, as a new see
            for his bishopric—*VCH Wilts*, III, 165
1225   Charter of Bishop Poore for the free citizens of the new
            city—Ballard & Tait, 45, 53, 85, 88
1227   Charter of Henry III creating a New S a free city—
            ibid, 2, 19, 29, 88, 116, 121, 247, 249, 256

Sherston   R

1404   Deeds referring to burgages—Wilts RO, 59

Tilshead   R

1086   Sixty-six burgesses paying the king 50s—DB, I, 65*a*

Tisbury   R

c 900   A *burh* with 500 hides assigned to it in the *Burghal
            Hidage*—Robertson, *Anglo-Saxon Charters*, 246. Mait-
            land and others doubted the identification and N.
            Brooks (*Med Archaeol*, VIII, 1964, 78) suggests Chisbury
            in Little Bedwyn, south-east of Marlborough

Trowbridge   R

1295–6   Burgesses paying relief on their burgages—PRO DL
            29/1/1

| Temp Edward I | More than forty burgages in a rental—PRO DL43/9/33 |

Warminster R

1086	Thirty burgesses—DB, i, 64d
1349	A portreeve; in fourteenth and fifteenth centuries a portmote—VCH Wilts, VIII, 128
1362	Portmote mentioned—Cal Pat Rolls, 1361-4, 163

Westbury S

1361	Portmote mentioned in inquest on Sir John Paveley, Lord of the manor—Cal Pat Rolls, 1361-4, 162-4
1375	Rents from burgages—PRO C135/249/7
1448	Parliamentary borough

Wilton R

897	A shire town—Anglo-Saxon Chronicle
c 900	A burh with 1,400 hides assigned to it in the Burghal Hidage—Robertson, Anglo-Saxon Charters, 246
1086	A borough paying the king £50—DB, I, 64c
1129 × 1135	Writ of Henry I conferring the customs of Winchester and London on his burgesses of the merchant guild or W—Ballard, 12

Wootton Bassett S

| 1236 | Burgesses mentioned—Cal Close Rolls, 1234-7, 223 |
| 1332 | Mentioned as borough—PRO SC 6/1057 3 |

WORCESTERSHIRE

Bewdley S

1367   Grant of a burgage in B—Birmingham Ref Lib, Deed no 488468

1472   Charter of Edward IV granting to the burgesses and inhabitants of B that they shall be a body corporate—*Cal Pat Rolls, 1467–77,* 361

Broadway E

1388   Court Roll mentions portmoot and burgages—PRO SC 2/210/25

1397   Claim by Joan Berton that her burgage had been freed by the burgesses of the borough from payment of heriot; she produces a charter of the portmoot—*VCH Worcs,* IV, 37

Clifton-upon-Teme S

1270   Charter of Henry III for Roger Mortimer, creating his vill of C a free borough—Ballard & Tait, 3, 132, 247, 249

Droitwich R

The Roman *Salinae*

1086   Eighteen burgesses paying 4s 6d—DB, 1, 174; thirty-one paying 15s 8d (174*b*); nine paying 30s (176); eleven paying 32 measures of salt (176*b*); twenty paying 50 measures (177)

1215   Charter of King John granting to the burgesses of Wich the right to hold the town in fee-farm, also a market and fair—Ballard, 115, 124, 175, 190, 216, 231

Dudley   S

1221   Represented as a borough, vill, and manor by a jury
            of its own at the eyre—PRO JI 1/1021 m 9*d*
1261   Agreement by Roger de Somery that the dean of
            Wolverhampton may establish a market on condition
            that he and his burgesses of D may be free of toll there
            —*Staffs Hist Coll*, IV (1), 1883, 251

Evesham   E

1055   Grant by Edward the Confessor of a port and market at
            E—*Chronicon Abbatiae de Evesham*, Rolls Ser, XXIX, 75
1221   Represented as a borough and vill by its own jury at
            the eyre—PRO JI 1/1021 m 8

Halesowen   E

1216 × 1272 Inspeximus by the abbot and convent of H of the
            charter of Henry III empowering them to make a
            borough with the privileges of Hereford—I. S. Jeayes.
            *Descriptive Catalogue of the Charters and Muniments of
            the Lyttleton Family*, 1893, 9–10

Kidderminster   S

ND (early   Grant of a burgage to Maiden Bradley—*VCH Worcs*,
thirteenth   IV, 163
cent)
ND (thirteenth Charter of John fitz John fitz Philip allowing all his
cent)   burgesses of Kinver to hold their burgages as freely as
                the burgesses of K hold theirs—S. Shaw. *Staffordshire*,
                II, 1801, 262
1254   Enfeoffment of a burgage—*VCH Worcs*, IV, 163

Pershore   E

1086   Twenty-eight burgesses paying 30s; toll yielding 10s—
            DB, I, 174c, 175
1221   Represented as a borough and vill by its own jury at
            the eyre—PRO JI 1/1221 m 7d

Tenbury   S

1455   Seven burgages mentioned in inquest on Sir Thomas
            Clifford—*VCH Worcs*, IV, 364

Worcester   R–E

680   An episcopal see
884 × 901   Charter of Aethelred and Aethelflaed of Mercia grant-
            ing to the bishop of W half the rights in the market
            and streets and half the land-rent—Birch, *Cart Sax*,
            no 579
1086   Market, mint, and burgesses—DB, I, 172a, 173c, 176b,
            178a, 177c, 180c
1189   Charter of Richard I allowing his burgesses of W to
            hold the town in fee-farm—Ballard, 222

YORKSHIRE

York   R–E

            The Roman *Eboracum*
625   An episcopal see
1066   A city divided into seven 'shires', six belonging to the
            king, one to the archbishop—DB, I, 298a
c 1130   Liberties of York granted to burgesses of Beverley—
            Ballard, 23, 99, 176, 191, 202

1154 × 1158 Charter of Henry II granting to the citizens of Y their merchant guild and all the liberties they had under Henry I—Ballard, 6, 204

1396 Incorporated as a county borough—Weinbaum, 132

See also Bootham and St Olave's Borough, North Riding (pp 186 and 188)

(EAST RIDING)

Beverley   E

1115–28 Charter of Thurstan, Archbishop of York, granting to the burgesses of B all the liberties of York—Ballard, 23, 99, 176, 191, 202

Bridlington

1086 Four burgesses paying rent—DB, I, 299*b*

Brough-on-Humber   E

1239 Grant by Walter, Archbishop of York, to his burgesses of B-on-H of burgage plots at a yearly rent of 4d, with the liberties of Beverley—*Surtees Soc*, LVI, 1870, 251

Hedon   S

1167 × 1170 Grant by Henry II to William, Earl of Albemarle, allowing his burgesses of H to hold in free burgage—Ballard, 38

1348 Incorporated—Weinbaum, 126

Howden   E

1311 One of the boroughs of the bishop of Durham in an account of the temporalities, *sede vacante*—PRO SC 6/1144/17

Kingston upon Hull   R

1299   Charter of Edward I creating a free borough with
                market, fair, coroner, and other privileges—Ballard &
                Tait, 6, 28, 93, 133, 140, 155, 160, 170, 172, 247, 249,
                360, 366
1440   Incorporated—Weinbaum, 128

Pocklington   R

1086   The king has four 'censores' paying 30s, and fifteen
                burgesses having seven ploughs—DB, I, 299c

Ravenserodd   R

1294   Taxed as a borough; 1307, 1313 as vill; 1315 onwards
                as borough—Willard, 435
1299   Charter of Edward I creating R a free borough with
                the same privileges as Hull—Ballard & Tait, 6, 28, 93,
                133, 140, 155, 160, 170, 247, 249, 360, 366

Skipsea   S

1160 × 1175   Land in the borough of S given to the monks of Brid-
                lington—W. Farrer. *Early Yorkshire Charters*, III, 1914,
                72
1260   Three burgage-holders enumerated—*Yorkshire In-
                quisitions*, I, Yorks Arch Soc Rec Ser, XII, 1892, 82

(NORTH RIDING)

Bootham   E

1275   Declared to be a free borough belonging to St Mary's
                Abbey—*VCH City of York*, 39, 40
1313, 1319,   Taxed as a borough—Willard, 435
   1322

Helmsley S

1186 × 1227   Charter of Robert de Ros granting to his burgesses of H all the liberties of York for 11 pounds of silver yearly —Ballard & Tait, 18, 63, 70, 304

Kirkby Moorside R

1154 × 1179   Charter of Henry II referring to K as one of his demesne boroughs—*Cal Pat Rolls, 1345–8*, 200

New Malton R

1154 × 1179   Charter of Henry II referring to M as one of his demesne boroughs—*Cal Pat Rolls, 1345–8*, 200

1184   .   Burgesses tallaged—*Pipe Roll Soc*, XXVII, 1915, 91

Northallerton E

1298   Parliamentary borough but not again until 1641— *VCH Yorks NR*, I, 422–3

1336   Two messuages held in free burgage from the bishop of Durham—*Cal Inq Post Mortem*, VII, 19

Pickering R

1100 × 1134   King John orders (1200) that the men of Pickering shall have their customs as under Henry I and Henry II— *Cal Rot Chart, 1199–1216*, 41

1205–6   Tallage paid by the borough—*Pipe Roll Soc*, NS, XX, 1942, 207

Richmond S

1093 × 1136   Charter (1136 × 1145) of Count Alan III, granting to his burgesses all the liberties they held by the charters of his father, Count Stephen, and his uncle, Count

Alan II (1089–93)—C. T. Clay. *Early Yorkshire Charters*, IV, 1935, 22–3

1136 × 1145   Grant by the same to the same of the site where the borough was built (*Fontenais*) and of the borough in fee-farm for £29 a year—ibid, 22

St Olave's Borough (York)   S

1088–93   William II confirmed Count Alan the Red of Brittany's grant to St Mary's abbey of the borough in which the church (of St Olave) is situated from *Galmonhou* towards Clifton and the water—W. Farrer, ed. *Early Yorks Charters*, I, 1914, 265, 270

Scarborough   R

1155   Charter of Henry II granting to his burgesses of S all the liberties and customs of York—Ballard, 25, 47

1485   Incorporated as a county borough—Weinbaum, 131

Skelton   S

1240   Peter de Brus confirms property in free burgage—*Guisborough Cartulary*, I (Surtees Soc, LXXXVI, 1889), 215

1274   Inquisition post mortem refers to the borough of S and pleas of its court—*Yorkshire Inquisitions*, I, Yorks Arch Soc Rec Ser, XII, 1892, 140

1335   Burgages in S—*Guisborough Cartulary*, I, 1889, 228

Stokesley   S

1347   Quitclaim of a burgage in S—*VCH Yorks NR*, II, 304

1382   John de Kilby leaves his burgages in S to his son—ibid

Thirsk ?R

1145   Charter of Roger de Mowbray granting to the priory of Newburgh, *inter alia*, the tofts and crofts in the borough of (East) T, and the chapel of St James—Dugdale, *Monasticon*, VI, 318

Whitby E

c 1128   Charter of Henry I granting to the abbey of W a burgage in W—PRO C52/CC7

1177 × 1189   Charter of Richard, Abbot of W, granting rights of free burgage to the inhabitants of W—Ballard, 39, 47, 69, 70, 113, 142

1201   Charter of King John disallowing the above—ibid, 36

Yarm

1273   Twelve carucates of land within the borough of Y—*Cal Close Rolls, 1272–9*, 46

(WEST RIDING)

Almondbury S

1357   Burgages in reeve's account—PRO DL29/507/5226

Bawtry S

1223 × 1238   Charter of Robert de Vipont, confirmed by Idonea, his widow, creating a borough at B—J. Hunter. *South Yorkshire*, 1868, 70

Bingley S

1273   Burgesses at B pay 36s 5d yearly—*Yorkshire Inquisitions*, I, Yorks Arch Soc Rec Ser, XII, 1892, 136

Boroughbridge   S

1165	2 marks paid *de ponte Burc*—*Pipe Roll Soc*, VIII, 1887, 51
1169	2 marks paid by the burgesses of B—*Pipe Roll Soc*, XIII, 1890, 37
1313, 1316	Taxed at the urban rate as a borough; 1319, 1332; 1334 as a vill—Willard, 435

Bradford   S

1311	£1 17s 6d paid in rents from 28⅔ and ⅛ burgages—PRO C134/22
1327	46s 2½d in rent of burgesses—PRO SC 6/1085/17

Doncaster   R

1194	Charter of Richard I granting to his burgesses of D their soke, with the right to hold the vill of D for 5 marks in addition to the ancient farm—Ballard, 223
1467	Incorporated—Weinbaum, 126

Drax   S

c 1250	£7 4s 4d collected in rents from the borough—*Yorkshire Inquisitions*, I, Yorks Arch Soc Rec Ser, XII, 1892, 124–5

Harewood   S

1266–7	Reeve of the borough—PRO SC 6/1077/26 m 1

Knaresborough

1168–9	Burgesses—*Pipe Roll Soc*, XIII, 1890, 37
1305	86 burgages—PRO E372/152*b* m 23
1313, 1316	Taxed as a borough; styled vill 1315, 1319, 1332, 1334, 1336—Willard, 435

Leeds S

1207   Charter of Maurice Paynel granting to his burgesses of
L all the liberties and free customs of Pontefract—
Ballard, 29, 41, 48, 51, 66, 73, 92, 97, 103, 119, 139,
140, 146, 148, 154, 163, 167, 179, 193, 215, 236, 249

Otley S

1304   Burgages and court of the borough mentioned—
PRO SC 6/1144/1 and E372/152B m 16

Pontefract S

1086   Ilbert de Lacy has sixty 'small burgesses' in his manor
of Tanshelf—DB, I, 316c

1154–8   Borough and market place mentioned in grant—W.
Farrer, ed. *Early Yorks Charters*, III, 1916, 1,499, 1,523

1194   Charter of Roger de Lacy granting to his burgesses of
P the liberties and free customs of the king's burgesses
of Grimsby—Ballard, 29, 41, 48, 51, 66, 73, 102, 119,
138, 140, 146, 147, 154, 163, 167, 179, 193, 215, 236,
249

1484   Incorporated—Weinbaum, 129
See also Westcheap (p 192)

Ripon E

1316   Recorded as a borough belonging to the archbishop of
York—PRO SC 6/1141/1

1341   186½ burgages—*Yorks Arch Jnl*, XXXII, 1934, 56

Sheffield S

1297   Charter of Thomas de Furnival granting to his free
tenants of the vill of S the fee-farm of all their tofts,
lands, and tenements—Ballard & Tait, 198, 220, 268,
323

Skipton

1266	Mentioned as borough—PRO SC 6/1087/6
1323	Borough court—PRO SC 6/1147/32a
1324	A burgage in *le Neumarket*—ibid, 32b

Tickhill   S

1086	In Dadsley thirty-one burgesses, three mills, and a church—DB, I, 319a
1340	Described as the borough of T—PRO SC 11/544

Wakefield   S

1180	Charter of Hamelin, Earl of Warenne, and Isabella, his wife, to the free burgesses of W, granting to each one toft and an acre of land in free burgage for 6d yearly——J. W. Walker. *Wakefield*, 1934, 53, from BM Lansdowne MS 972

Westcheap (Pontefract)   S

1255 × 1258	Charter by Edmund, Earl of Lincoln, granting to his men dwelling in Westcheap near Tanshelf the same liberties and customs as his other burgesses of Pontefract—Ballard & Tait, 41

ADDENDA

The search for evidence of burghality is a continuing one, and readers are invited to send any further references to Professor M. W. Beresford, The University, Leeds, 2; these will be acknowledged in any further publication.

The information below has come to light during the course of publication in the Spring of 1973.

CHESHIRE

Malpas

c 1280   Grant of a burgage—Chesh RO, DCH/C/250

STAFFORDSHIRE

Alrewas

1328   Burgage tenure mentioned in court roll—Staffs RO, WSL D/O 3

Newcastle-under-Lyme

1179   Liberties of N-u-L granted to Preston, Lancs—Ballard, 27. Dr Palliser reports that none of the copies of the alleged 1173 charter are of that date; see also I. H. Jeayes in *The Preston Guardian*, 23 July 1910

Authors' Acknowledgements

Cheshire: Dr R. E. Yarwood; *Northumberland:* Mr L. C. Coombes, Mr J. Godwin; *Warws:* Mr. H. J. Usher; *Yorks:* Mr B. J. D. Harrison.

INDEX